JULIUS CÆSAR

WILLIAM SHAKESPEARE

SCHOLASTIC BOOK SERVICES
New York Toronto London Auckland Sydney Tokyo

This text of *Julius Caesar* is based on the First Folio of 1623 and the act-scene division of the Globe edition of 1874, edited and annotated by the editors of Scholastic.

ISBN: 0-590-36100-7

12 11 10 9 8 7 6 5   4 5 6/8

Printed in the U.S.A.   06

CAST OF CHARACTERS

JULIUS CAESAR

OCTAVIUS CAESAR
MARCUS ANTONIUS · *triumvirs after the death*
M. AEMILIUS LEPIDUS · *of Julius Caesar*

CICERO
PUBLIUS · *senators*
POPILIUS LENA

MARCUS BRUTUS
CASSIUS
CASCA
TREBONIUS · *conspirators against*
LIGARIUS · *Julius Caesar*
DECIUS BRUTUS
METELLUS CIMBER
CINNA

FLAVIUS *and* MARULLUS, *tribunes of the people*
ARTEMIDORUS, *a teacher*
SOOTHSAYER
CINNA, *a poet*
ANOTHER POET

LUCILIUS
TITINIUS
MESSALA · *friends to Brutus and Cassius*
YOUNG CATO
VOLUMNIUS

VARRO
CLITUS
CLAUDIUS
STRATO · *servants to Brutus*
LUCIUS
DARDANIUS

PINDARUS, *servant to Cassius*
A SERVANT *to Caesar; to Antony; to Octavius*
CALPURNIA, *wife of Caesar*
PORTIA, *wife of Brutus*
GHOST OF CAESAR
SENATORS, CITIZENS, GUARDS, SOLDIERS, &C.

SCENE: *Rome; near Sardis; near Philippi*

TIME: 44 B.C.

ACT ONE, SCENE ONE

ROME. A public place. Enter Flavius, Marullus, and Citizens.

FLAVIUS

Hence! Home, you idle creatures, get you home.
Is this a holiday? What, know you not,
Being mechanical,[1] you ought not walk
Upon a laboring day without the sign [2]
Of your profession? Speak, what trade art thou?

FIRST CITIZEN

Why, sir, a carpenter.

MARULLUS

Where is thy leather apron and thy rule?
What dost thou with thy best apparel on?
You, sir, what trade are you?

SECOND CITIZEN

Truly, sir, in respect of a fine workman, I am but,   10
as you would say, a cobbler.

MARULLUS

But what trade are thou? Answer me directly.

[1] workmen   [2] clothes, tools

1

SECOND CITIZEN

A trade, sir, that I hope I may use with a safe
conscience; which is indeed, sir, a mender of bad
soles.[3]

FLAVIUS

What trade, thou knave? Thou naughty knave,
what trade?

SECOND CITIZEN

Nay, I beseech you, sir, be not out with me; yet
if you be out, sir, I can mend you.

MARULLUS

What meanest thou by that? Mend me, thou
saucy fellow?

SECOND CITIZEN

Why, sir, cobble you.   20

FLAVIUS

Thou art a cobbler, art thou?

SECOND CITIZEN

Truly, sir, all that I live by is with the awl. I
meddle with no tradesman's matters, nor women's
matters, but with awl. I am indeed, sir, a surgeon
to old shoes. When they are in great danger, I
recover them. As proper [4] men as ever trod upon
neat's leather [5] have gone upon my handiwork.

---

[3] *The second citizen puns on the words "sole" (soul)
and—later—"awl" (all).*   [4] handsome   [5] cowhide

2

But wherefore art not in thy shop today?
Why dost thou lead these men about the streets?

SECOND CITIZEN

Truly, sir, to wear out their shoes, to get myself   30
into more work. But indeed, sir, we make holiday
to see Caesar and to rejoice in his triumph.

MARULLUS

Wherefore rejoice? What conquest brings he
    home?
What tributaries [6] follow him to Rome,
To grace in captive bonds his chariot wheels?
You blocks, you stones, you worse than senseless
    things!
O you hard hearts, you cruel men of Rome,
Knew you not Pompey? [7] Many a time and oft
Have you climbed up to walls and battlements,
To towers and windows, yea, to chimney tops,   40
Your infants in your arms, and there have sat
The livelong day, with patient expectation,
To see great Pompey pass the streets of Rome.
And when you saw his chariot but appear,
Have you not made an universal shout,
That Tiber trembled underneath her banks,
To hear the replication [8] of your sounds
Made in her concave shores?
And do you now put on your best attire?
And do you now cull out a holiday? [9]   50
And do you now strew flowers in his way,

---

[6] captives [7] *Pompey (106-48 B.C.), a great Roman
leader and general, lost in civil war to Caesar at Pharsalia,
48 B.C.* [8] echo [9] *Cull . . . holiday:* make a new holiday

3

That comes in triumph over Pompey's blood?
Be gone!
Run to your houses, fall upon your knees,
Pray to the gods to intermit [10] the plague
That needs must light on this ingratitude.

FLAVIUS

Go, go, good countrymen, and for this fault,
Assemble all the poor men of your sort;
Draw them to Tiber banks, and weep your tears
Into the channel till the lowest stream   60
Do kiss the most exalted shores of all.

Exeunt Citizens.

See whether their basest mettle [11] be not moved;
They vanish tongue-tied in their guiltiness.
Go you down that way towards the Capitol;
This way will I. Disrobe the images [12]
If you do find them decked with ceremonies.[13]

MARULLUS

May we do so?
You know it is the feast of Lupercal.[14]

FLAVIUS

It is no matter. Let no images
Be hung with Caesar's trophies. I'll about,   70
And drive away the vulgar from the streets.
So do you too, where you perceive them thick.
These growing feathers plucked from Caesar's
    wing

[10] put off   [11] nature   [12] statues   [13] ornaments
[14] *Lupercal was a fertility festival honoring the god Lupercus, whose Greek name was Pan.*

4

Will make him fly an ordinary pitch,[15]
Who else would soar above the view of men
And keep us all in servile fearfulness.

Exeunt.

ACT ONE, SCENE TWO

*The same. Music. Enter Caesar, Antony
dressed for the course, Calpurnia, Portia,
Decius, Cicero, Brutus, Cassius, and
Casca. Soothsayer and Citizens, Flavius
and Marullus follow.*

CAESAR

Calpurnia.

CASCA

Peace ho! Caesar speaks.

Music ceases.

CAESAR

Calpurnia.

CALPURNIA

Here, my lord.

CAESAR

Stand you directly in Antonius' way
When he doth run his course. Antonius.

ANTONY

Caesar, my lord?

[15] height

5

CAESAR

Forget not in your speed, Antonius,
To touch Calpurnia; for our elders say
The barren, touched in this holy chase,
Shake off their sterile curse.

ANTONY

                    I shall remember.
When Caesar says "Do this," it is performed.   **10**

CAESAR

Set on, and leave no ceremony out.   *Music.*

SOOTHSAYER

Caesar!

CAESAR

Ha! Who calls?

CASCA

Bid every noise be still. Peace yet again!

                      Music ceases.

CAESAR

Who is it in the press [1] that calls on me?
I hear a tongue shriller than all the music
Cry "Caesar!" Speak: Caesar is turned to hear.

SOOTHSAYER

Beware the ides [2] of March.

CAESAR

                  What man is that?

[1] crowd   [2] *The ides were the mid-point in the month.*

BRUTUS

A soothsayer bids you beware the ides of March.

CAESAR

Set him before me. Let me see his face.   20

CASSIUS

Fellow, come from the throng. Look upon Caesar.

CAESAR

What sayest thou to me now? Speak once again.

SOOTHSAYER

Beware the ides of March.

CAESAR

He is a dreamer. Let us leave him. Pass.

> *Trumpets. Exeunt all*
> *but Brutus and Cassius.*

CASSIUS

Will you go see the order of the course? [3]

BRUTUS

Not I.

CASSIUS

I pray you do.

BRUTUS

I am not gamesome. [4] I do lack some part

[3] *order of the course*: how the race is going
[4] sport-loving, competitive

Of that quick spirit that is in Antony.
Let me not hinder, Cassius, your desires;   30
I'll leave you.

CASSIUS

Brutus, I do observe you now of late:
I have not from your eyes that gentleness
And show of love as I was wont to have.
You bear too stubborn [5] and too strange a hand
Over your friend that loves you.

BRUTUS

                              Cassius,
Be not deceived. If I have veiled my look,
I turn the trouble of my countenance
Merely upon myself. Vexed I am
Of late with passions of some difference,[6]   40
Conceptions only proper to myself,
Which give some soil, perhaps, to my behaviors.
But let not therefore my good friends be
   grieved—
Among which number, Cassius, be you one—
Nor construe any further my neglect
Than that poor Brutus, with himself at war,
Forgets the shows of love to other men.

CASSIUS

Then, Brutus, I have much mistook your passion,
By means whereof this breast of mine hath buried
Thoughts of great value, worthy cogitations.   50
Tell me, good Brutus, can you see your face?

BRUTUS

No, Cassius, for the eye sees not itself

[5] harsh   [6] *passions . . . difference:* conflicting emotions

But by reflection, by some other things.

CASSIUS

'Tis just,
And it is very much lamented, Brutus,
That you have no such mirrors as will turn
Your hidden worthiness into your eye,
That you might see your shadow. I have heard
Where many of the best respect in Rome—
Except immortal Caesar—speaking of Brutus   60
And groaning underneath this age's yoke,
Have wished that noble Brutus had his eyes.[7]

BRUTUS

Into what dangers would you lead me, Cassius,
That you would have me seek into myself
For that which is not in me?

CASSIUS

Therefore, good Brutus, be prepared to hear.
And since you know you cannot see yourself
So well as by reflection, I, your glass,
Will modestly discover [8] to yourself
That of yourself which you yet know not of.   70
And be not jealous on [9] me, gentle Brutus.
Were I a common laugher, or did use
To stale [10] with ordinary oaths my love
To every new protester; if you know
That I do fawn on men, and hug them hard,
And after scandal[11] them; or if you know
That I profess myself in banqueting

[7] *Have . . . eyes*: many have wished that Brutus could
see as they did   [8] reveal   [9] suspicious of   [10] cheapen
[11] slander

9

To all the rout,[12] then hold me dangerous.

Flourish and shout.

BRUTUS

What means this shouting? I do fear the people
Choose Caesar for their king.

CASSIUS

Ay, do you fear it?   80
Then must I think you would not have it so.

BRUTUS

I would not, Cassius; yet I love him well.
But wherefore do you hold me here so long?
What is it that you would impart to me?
If it be aught toward the general good,
Set honor in one eye, and death i' the other,
And I will look on both indifferently,[13]
For let the gods so speed me as I love
The name of honor more than I fear death.

CASSIUS

I know that virtue to be in you, Brutus,   90
As well as I do know your outward favor.
Well, honor is the subject of my story.
I cannot tell what you and other men
Think of this life; but for my single self,
I had as lief not be, as live to be
In awe of such a thing as I myself.[14]
I was born free as Caesar; so were you.

[12] *if . . . rout*: if you think my friendship is so cheap
that I make friends with everyone at a banquet
[13] impartially   [14] *I had . . . myself*: I would rather
not exist than be afraid of another man

10

We both have fed as well, and we can both
Endure the winter's cold as well as he.
For once, upon a raw and gusty day,   **100**
The troubled Tiber chafing with her shores,
Caesar said to me "Darest thou, Cassius, now
Leap in with me into this angry flood
And swim to yonder point?" Upon the word,
Accoutred [15] as I was, I plunged in
And bade him follow. So indeed he did.
The torrent roared, and we did buffet it
With lusty sinews, throwing it aside
And stemming it with hearts of controversy. [16]
But ere we could arrive the point proposed,   **110**
Caesar cried "Help me, Cassius, or I sink."
I, as Aeneas, [17] our great ancestor,
Did from the flames of Troy upon his shoulder
The old Anchises bear, so from the waves of
    Tiber
Did I the tired Caesar. And this man
Is now become a god, and Cassius is
A wretched creature and must bend his body
If Caesar carelessly but nod on him.
He had a fever when he was in Spain,
And when the fit was on him, I did mark   **120**
How he did shake. 'Tis true, this god did shake.
His coward lips did from their color fly,
And that same eye, whose bend [18] doth awe the
    world,
Did lose its luster; I did hear him groan.
Ay, and that tongue of his, that bade the Romans
Mark him and write his speeches in their books,

[15] armed   [16] rivalry   [17] *Aeneas, founder of the
Roman state, carried his father Anchises on his back
away from the burning city of Troy.*   [18] gaze

"Alas," it cried, "give me some drink, Titinius,"
As a sick girl. Ye gods, it doth amaze me
A man of such a feeble temper should
So get the start of the majestic world   **130**
And bear the palm [19] alone.   *Shout and flourish.*

Another general shout?
I do believe that these applauses are
For some new honors that are heaped on Caesar.

Why, man, he doth bestride the narrow world
Like a Colossus,[20] and we petty men
Walk under his huge legs and peep about
To find ourselves dishonorable graves.
Men at some time are masters of their fates.
The fault, dear Brutus, is not in our stars,   **140**
But in ourselves, that we are underlings.
"Brutus," and "Caesar." What should be in that
   "Caesar"?
Why should that name be sounded more than
   yours?
Write them together: yours is as fair a name.
Sound them: it doth become the mouth as well.
Weigh them: it is as heavy. Conjure with 'em:
"Brutus" will start a spirit [21] as soon as "Caesar."
Now in the names of all the gods at once,
Upon what meat doth this our Caesar feed,
That he is grown so great? Age, thou art shamed.   **150**
Rome, thou hast lost the breed of noble bloods.
When went there by an age, since the great flood,

19 prize   20 huge statue   21 *start a spirit:* raise up a ghost

But it was famed with more than with one man?
When could they say—till now—that talked of
 Rome,
That her wide walls encompassed but one man?
Now is it Rome indeed, and room enough,
When there is in it but one only man.
O you and I have heard our fathers say
There was a Brutus [22] once that would have
 brooked
Th' eternal devil to keep his state in Rome   160
As easily as a king.[23]

BRUTUS

That you do love me, I am nothing jealous.[24]
What you would work me to, I have some aim.[25]
How I have thought of this, and of these times,
I shall recount hereafter. For this present,
I would not—so with love I might entreat you—
Be any further moved. What you have said
I will consider. What you have to say
I will with patience hear, and find a time
Both meet [26] to hear and answer such high things.   170
Till then, my noble friend, chew upon this:
Brutus had rather be a villager
Than to repute himself a son of Rome
Under these hard conditions as this time
Is like to lay upon us.

[22] Lucius Junius Brutus, Marcus Brutus' ancestor,
helped to drive out the Tarquinians, early Roman tyrants,
and to found the Roman Republic (509 B.C.).
[23] that . . . king: who would have tolerated the devil's
rule in Rome as soon as the rule of a king
[24] doubtful [25] inkling, idea [26] fitting

13

CASSIUS

                    I am glad
That my weak words have struck but [27] this much
    show
Of fire from Brutus.

Enter Caesar and his Train.

BRUTUS

The games are done, and Caesar is returning.

CASSIUS

As they pass by, pluck Casca by the sleeve,
And he will, after his sour fashion, tell you   180
What hath proceeded worthy note today.

BRUTUS

I will do so. But look you, Cassius,
The angry spot doth glow on Caesar's brow,
And all the rest look like a chidden train.[28]
Calpurnia's cheek is pale, and Cicero
Looks with such ferret and such fiery eyes
As we have seen him in the Capitol,
Being crossed in conference by some senators.

CASSIUS

Casca will tell us what the matter is.

CAESAR

Antonius.   190

ANTONY

Caesar?

27 even   28 *chidden train:* scolded followers

14

CAESAR

Let me have men about me that are fat.
Sleek-headed men, and such as sleep o' nights.
Yond Cassius has a lean and hungry look;
He thinks too much. Such men are dangerous.

ANTONY

Fear him not, Caesar; he's not dangerous.
He is a noble Roman, and well given.[29]

CAESAR

Would he were fatter! But I fear him not.
Yet if my name were liable to fear,
I do not know the man I should avoid   **200**
So soon as that spare Cassius. He reads much,
He is a great observer, and he looks
Quite through the deeds of men. He loves no
    plays
As thou dost, Antony; he hears no music;
Seldom he smiles, and smiles in such a sort [30]
As if he mocked himself and scorned his spirit
That could be moved to smile at anything.
Such men as he be never at heart's ease
Whiles they behold a greater than themselves,
And therefore are they very dangerous.   **210**
I rather tell thee what is to be feared
Than what I fear; for always I am Caesar.
Come on my right hand, for this ear is deaf,
And tell me truly what thou thinkest of him.

> *Trumpets sound.*
> *Exeunt Caesar and all his Train but Casca.*

[29] disposed   [30] way

15

CASCA

You pulled me by the cloak. Would you speak
  with me?

BRUTUS

Ay, Casca, tell us what hath chanced today
That Caesar looks so sad.[31]

CASCA

Why, you were with him, were you not?

BRUTUS

I should not then ask Casca what had chanced.

CASCA

Why, there was a crown offered him; and being   **220**
offered him, he put it by with the back of his
hand thus, and then the people fell a-shouting.

BRUTUS

What was the second noise for?

CASCA

Why, for that too.

CASSIUS

They shouted thrice. What was the last cry for?

CASCA

Why, for that too.

BRUTUS

Was the crown offered him thrice?

[31] solemn

16

CASCA

Ay, marry, was't! And he put it by thrice, every
time gentler than other; and at every putting by
mine honest neighbors shouted.   230

CASSIUS

Who offered him the crown?

CASCA

Why, Antony.

BRUTUS

Tell us the manner of it, gentle Casca.

CASCA

I can as well be hanged as tell the manner of it.
It was mere foolery; I did not mark it. I saw
Mark Antony offer him a crown, yet 'twas not a
crown neither, 'twas one of these coronets;[32] and,
as I told you, he put it by once: but for all
that, to my thinking he would fain have had it.
Then he offered it to him again; then he put it   240
by again, but to my thinking he was very loth to
lay his fingers off it. And then he offered it the
third time; he put it the third time by, and still
as he refused it the rabblement hooted, and
clapped their chopped [33] hands, and threw up
their sweaty night-caps, and uttered such a deal
of stinking breath because Caesar refused the
crown that it had almost choked Caesar; for he
swounded,[34] and fell down at it. And for my
own part, I durst not laugh, for fear of opening   250
my lips and receiving the bad air.

[32] small, laurel-wreathed crowns   [33] chapped   [34] fainted

17

CASSIUS

But soft, I pray you. What, did Caesar swound?

CASCA

He fell down in the market place, and foamed at mouth, and was speechless.

BRUTUS

'Tis very like he hath the falling sickness.[35]

CASSIUS

No, Caesar hath it not; but you, and I,
And honest Casca, we have the falling sickness.

CASCA

I know not what you mean by that, but I am sure
Caesar fell down. If the tag-rag [36] people did not
clap him and hiss him, according as he pleased   260
and displeased them, as they used to do the
players in the theater, I am no true man.

BRUTUS

What said he when he came unto himself?

CASCA

Marry, before he fell down, when he perceived
the common herd was glad he refused the crown,
he plucked me ope [37] his doublet and offered
them his throat to cut. An [38] I had been a man
of any occupation, if I would not have taken him
at a word I would I might go to hell among the
rogues. And so he fell. When he came to himself   270

35 epilepsy   36 gypsy-like   37 *plucked me ope:* pulled open
38 If

18

again, he said if he had done or said anything amiss, he desired their worships to think it was his infirmity. Three or four wenches where I stood cried "Alas, good soul!" and forgave him with all their hearts. But there's no heed to be taken of them. If Caesar had stabbed their mothers, they would have done no less.

BRUTUS

And after that, he came thus sad away?

CASCA

Ay.

CASSIUS

Did Cicero say anything?   280

CASCA

Ay, he spoke Greek.

CASSIUS

To what effect?

CASCA

Nay, an I tell you that, I'll ne'er look you i' th' face again. But those that understood him smiled at one another, and shook their heads; but for mine own part, it was Greek [39] to me. I could tell you more news too. Marullus and Flavius, for pulling scarfs off Caesar's images, are put to silence. Fare you well. There was more foolery yet, if I could remember it.   290

[39] *i.e.*, incomprehensible

19

CASSIUS

Will you sup with me tonight, Casca?

CASCA

No, I am promised forth.

CASSIUS

Will you dine with me tomorrow?

CASCA

Ay, if I be alive, and your mind hold,[40] and your
dinner worth the eating.

CASSIUS

Good. I will expect you.

CASCA

Do so. Farewell both.   *Exit.*

BRUTUS

What a blunt fellow is this grown to be!
He was quick mettle [41] when he went to school.

CASSIUS

So is he now in execution   300
Of any bold or noble enterprise,
However he puts on this tardy form.[42]
This rudeness is a sauce to his good wit,
Which gives men stomach to digest his words
With better appetite.

---

[40] doesn't change   [41] quick-witted
[42] *tardy form:* sluggish pose

BRUTUS

And so it is. For this time I will leave you.
Tomorrow, if you please to speak with me,
I will come home to you; or if you will,
Come home to me, and I will wait for you.

CASSIUS

I will do so. Till then, think of the world.   310

Exit Brutus.

Well, Brutus, thou art noble; yet I see
Thy honorable mettle may be wrought [43]
From that it is disposed. Therefore it is meet
That noble minds keep ever with their likes,
For who so firm that cannot be seduced?
Caesar doth bear me hard,[44] but he loves Brutus.
If I were Brutus now, and he were Cassius,
He [45] should not humor me. I will this night,
In several hands,[46] in at his windows throw,
As if they came from several citizens,   320
Writings all tending to the great opinion
That Rome holds of his name, wherein obscurely
Caesar's ambition shall be glanced [47] at.
And after this let Caesar seat him sure,
For we will shake him, or worse days endure.

Exit.

[43] *Thy . . . wrought*: your honorable character may be
changed   [44] a grudge   [45] *i.e.*, Brutus   [46] handwritings
[47] hinted

21

ACT ONE, SCENE THREE

A street of Rome. Thunder and lightning.
Enter Casca and Cicero separately.

CICERO

Good even, Casca. Brought you Caesar home?
Why are you breathless, and why stare you so?

CASCA

Are you not moved, when all the sway [1] of earth
Shakes like a thing unfirm? O Cicero,
I have seen tempests when the scolding winds
Have rived the knotty oaks, and I have seen
The ambitious ocean swell and rage and foam
To be exalted with the threatening clouds;
But never till tonight, never till now,
Did I go through a tempest dropping fire.   10
Either there is a civil strife in heaven,
Or else the world, too saucy with the gods,
Incenses them to send destruction.

CICERO

Why, saw you anything more wonderful? [2]

CASCA

A common slave—you know him well by sight—
Held up his left hand, which did flame and burn
Like twenty torches joined; and yet his hand,
Not sensible of fire, remained unscorched.
Besides—I have not since put up my sword—
Against [3] the Capitol I met a lion,   20
Who glared upon me and went surly by
Without annoying me. And there were drawn
Upon a heap [4] a hundred ghastly women,

[1] order   [2] amazing   [3] opposite
[4] *drawn . . . heap:* huddling together

22

Transformed with their fear, who swore they saw
Men, all in fire, walk up and down the streets.
And yesterday the bird of night [5] did sit,
Even at noonday, upon the market place,
Hooting and shrieking. When these prodigies
Do so conjointly meet, [6] let not men say
"These are their reasons—they are natural."   30
For I believe they are portentous things
Unto the climate that they point upon.

CICERO

Indeed, it is a strange-disposed time.
But men may construe things after their fashion,
Clean from [7] the purpose of the things them-
    selves.
Comes Caesar to the Capitol tomorrow?

CASCA

He doth; for he did bid Antonius
Send word to you he would be there tomorrow.

CICERO

Good night then, Casca. This disturbed sky
Is not to walk in.

CASCA

      Farewell, Cicero. *Exit Cicero.*   40
      Enter Cassius.

CASSIUS

Who's there?

CASCA

A Roman.

[5] *i.e.,* owl [6] *When . . . meet:* when strange things
happen all at the same time [7] *clean from:* contrary to

23

CASSIUS

Casca, by your voice.

CASCA

Your ear is good. Cassius, what night is this!

CASSIUS

A very pleasing night to honest men.

CASCA

Who ever knew the heavens menace so?

CASSIUS

Those that have known the earth so full of faults.
For my part, I have walked about the streets,
Submitting me unto the perilous night;
And thus unbraced,[8] Casca, as you see,
Have bared my bosom to the thunder-stone;
And when the cross blue lightning seemed to
open   50
The breast of heaven, I did present myself
Even in the aim and very flash of it.

CASCA

But wherefore did you so much tempt the
heavens?
It is the part of men to fear and tremble
When the most mighty gods by tokens send
Such dreadful heralds to astonish us.

CASSIUS

You are dull, Casca, and those sparks of life

[8] unbuttoned

That should be in a Roman you do want,[9]
Or else you use not. You look pale, and gaze,
And put on fear, and cast yourself in wonder,   60
To see the strange impatience of the heavens.
But if you would consider the true cause—
Why all these fires, why all these gliding ghosts,
Why birds and beasts from quality and kind;
Why old men fool and children calculate,
Why all these things change from their
    ordinance,[10]
Their natures, and pre-formed faculties,
To monstrous quality—why you shall find
That heaven hath infused them with these spirits
To make them instruments of fear and warning   70
Unto some monstrous state.
Now could I, Casca, name to thee a man
Most like this dreadful night
That thunders, lightens, opens graves, and roars
As doth the lion in the Capitol—
A man no mightier than thyself or me
In personal action, yet prodigious grown
And fearful, as these strange eruptions are.

CASCA

'Tis Caesar that you mean, is it not, Cassius?

CASSIUS

Let it be who it is; for Romans now   80
Have thews [11] and limbs like to their ancestors;
But, woe the while! our fathers' minds are dead,
And we are governed with our mothers' spirits;
Our yoke and sufferance show us womanish.

[9] lack   [10] natural order   [11] sinews

25

CASCA

Indeed, they say the senators tomorrow
Mean to establish Caesar as a king,
And he shall wear his crown by sea and land
In every place save here in Italy.

CASSIUS

I know where I will wear this dagger then;
Cassius from bondage will deliver Cassius.   90
Therein, ye gods, you make the weak most strong;
Therein, ye gods, you tyrants do defeat.
Nor stony tower, nor walls of beaten brass,
Nor airless dungeon, nor strong links of iron,
Can be rententive to the strength of spirit;
But life, being weary of these worldly bars,
Never lacks power to dismiss itself.
If I know this, know all the world besides,
That part of tyranny that I do bear
I can shake off at pleasure.   *Thunder still.*

CASCA

                    So can I.   100
So every bondman in his own hand bears
The power to cancel his captivity.

CASSIUS

And why should Caesar be a tyrant then?
Poor man! I know he would not be a wolf,
But that he sees the Romans are but sheep;
He were no lion, were not Romans hinds.[12]
Those that with haste will make a mighty fire
Begin it with weak straws. What trash is Rome,

---

[12] does (female deer)

What rubbish, and what offal,[13] when it serves
For the base matter to illuminate   110
So vile a thing as Caesar! But, O grief,
Where hast thou led me? I perhaps speak this
Before a willing bondman; then I know
My answer must be made. But I am armed,
And dangers are to me indifferent.[14]

CASCA

You speak to Casca, and to such a man
That is no fleering [15] tell-tale. Hold, my hand.
Be factious [16] for redress of all these griefs,
And I will set this foot of mine as far
As who goes farthest.

CASSIUS

There's a bargain made.   120
Now know you, Casca, I have moved already
Some certain of the noblest-minded Romans
To undergo with me an enterprise
Of honorable-dangerous consequence;
And I do know, by this they stay [17] for me
In Pompey's Porch,[18] for now, this fearful night,
There is no stir or walking in the streets,
And the complexion of the element
Is favored [19] like the work we have in hand,
Most bloody, fiery, and most terrible.   130

Enter Cinna.

CASCA

Stand close awhile, for here comes one in haste.

13 refuse, garbage   14 of no concern   15 mocking   16 conspiring   17 wait   18 *entrance to Pompey's Theater*   19 *Is favored*: looks

27

CASSIUS

'Tis Cinna, I do know him by his gait.
He is a friend. Cinna, where haste you so?

CINNA

To find out you. Who's that? Metellus Cimber?

CASSIUS

No, it is Casca, one incorporate [20]
To our attempts. Am I not stayed for, Cinna?

CINNA

I am glad on't. What a fearful night is this!
There's two or three of us have seen strange
   sights.

CASSIUS

Am I not stayed for? Tell me.

CINNA

                  Yes, you are.
O Cassius, if you could   **140**
But win the noble Brutus to our party—

CASSIUS

Be you content. Good Cinna, take this paper,
And look you lay it in the praetor's chair
Where Brutus [21] may but find it. And throw this
In at his window. Set this up with wax
Upon old Brutus' statue. All this done,
Repair to Pompey's Porch, where you shall find
   us.

[20] part of   [21] *Brutus was a praetor, or judge, of Rome.*

28

Is Decius Brutus and Trebonius there?

CINNA

All but Metellus Cimber, and he's gone
To seek you at your house. Well, I will hie,[22]   **150**
And so bestow these papers as you bade me.

CASSIUS

That done, repair to Pompey's Theater.

Exit Cinna.

Come, Casca, you and I will yet ere day
See Brutus at his house. Three parts of him
Is ours already; and the man entire,
Upon the next encounter, yields him ours.[23]

CASCA

O he sits high in all the people's hearts;
And that which would appear offense in us,
His countenance,[24] like richest alchemy,
Will change to virtue and to worthiness.   **160**

CASSIUS

Him and his worth and our great need of him
You have right well conceited.[25] Let us go,
For it is after midnight; and ere day
We will awake him and be sure of him. *Exeunt.*

---

[22] hurry   [23] *yields . . . ours*: will come over to our side
[24] support   [25] expressed

ACT TWO, SCENE ONE

Rome. Brutus' house.
Brutus is in his orchard.

BRUTUS

What, Lucius, ho!
I cannot, by the progress of the stars,
Give guess how near to day. Lucius, I say!
I would it were my fault to sleep so soundly.
When, Lucius, when? Awake, I say. What,
    Lucius!

Enter Lucius.

LUCIUS

Called you, my lord?

BRUTUS

Get me a taper [1] in my study, Lucius.
When it is lighted, come and call me here.

LUCIUS

I will, my lord.   *Exit.*

BRUTUS

It must be by his death; and for my part,   **10**
I know no personal cause to spurn [2] at him,
But for the general. He would be crowned.
How that might change his nature, there's the
    question.
It is the bright day that brings forth the adder,
And that craves wary walking. Crown him that,[3]
And then I grant we put a sting in him
That at his will he may do danger with.

---

  [1] candle   [2] oppose   [3] *i.e.*, king

The abuse of greatness is when it disjoins
Remorse from power. And to speak truth of
　Caesar,
I have not known when his affections [4] swayed　　— 20
More than his reason. But 'tis a common proof
That lowliness is young ambition's [5] ladder,
Whereto the climber-upward turns his face.
But when he once attains the upmost round,
He then unto the ladder turns his back,
Looks in the clouds, scorning the base degrees [6]
By which he did ascend.—So Caesar may.
Then lest he may, prevent. And since the quarrel
Will bear no color for the thing he is,[7]
Fashion it thus [8]: that what he is, augmented,　　30
Would run to these and these extremities.
And therefore think him as a serpent's egg,
Which hatched, would as his kind grow mis-
　chievous;
And kill him in the shell.

Enter Lucius.

LUCIUS

The taper burneth in your closet, [9] sir.
Searching the window for a flint, I found
This paper, thus sealed up; and I am sure
It did not lie there when I went to bed.

Gives him the letter.

BRUTUS

Get you to bed again; it is not day.

[4] feelings　[5] *Here, and through the play, "ambition"
has the meaning of unnatural greed for power.*　[6] *Steps*
[7] *And . . . is:* since what Caesar is now gives us no
reason for opposing him　[8] *Fashion it thus:* put it this
way　[9] study

31

Is not tomorrow, boy, the ides of March?

LUCIUS

I know not, sir.

BRUTUS

Look in the calendar, and bring me word.

LUCIUS

I will, sir. *Exit.*

BRUTUS

The exhalations whizzing in the air
Give so much light that I may read by them.
Brutus, thou sleepest. Awake, and see thyself.
Shall Rome, etc. Speak, strike, redress.
"Brutus, thou sleepest. Awake!"
Such instigations have been often dropped
Where I have took them up.
"Shall Rome, etc." Thus must I piece [10] it out:
Shall Rome stand under one man's awe? What,
  Rome?
My ancestors did from the streets of Rome
The Tarquin drive, when he was called a king.
"Speak, strike, redress." Am I entreated
To speak and strike? O Rome, I make thee
  promise,
If the redress will follow, thou receivest
Thy full petition at the hand of Brutus.

Enter Lucius.

LUCIUS

Sir, March is wasted fifteen days.
                Knock within.

[10] figure

'Tis good. Go to the gate; somebody knocks.   **60**

Exit Lucius.

Since Cassius first did whet me against Caesar,
I have not slept.
Between the acting of a dreadful thing
And the first motion, all the interim is
Like a phantasma or a hideous dream.
The genius [11] and the mortal instruments [12]
Are then in council; and the state of man,
Like to a little kingdom, suffers then
The nature of an insurrection.

Enter Lucius.

LUCIUS

Sir, 'tis your brother [13] Cassius at the door,   **70**
Who doth desire to see you.

BRUTUS

                    Is he alone?

LUCIUS

No, sir, there are more with him.

BRUTUS

                    Do you know them?

LUCIUS

No, sir. Their hats are plucked about their ears
And half their faces buried in their cloaks,

[11] imagination   [12] body   [13] *i.e.*, friend

33

That by no means I may discover [14] them
By any mark of favor.[15]

Let 'em enter.

Exit Lucius.

They are the faction. O conspiracy,
Shamest thou to show thy dangerous brow by
   night,
When evils are most free? O then by day
Where wilt thou find a cavern dark enough   80
To mask thy monstrous visage? Seek none,
   conspiracy.
Hide it in smiles and affability.
For if thou put thy native semblance on,
Not Erebus [16] itself were dim enough
To hide thee from prevention.

   Enter Cassius, Casca, Decius, Cinna,
     Metellus Cimber, and Trebonius.

CASSIUS

I think we are too bold upon your rest.
Good morrow, Brutus. Do we trouble you?

BRUTUS

I have been up this hour, awake all night.
Know I these men that come along with you?

CASSIUS

Yes, every man of them; and no man here   90

---

[14] recognize [15] feature [16] *In Greek mythology, Ere-*
bus was a region of darkness between Earth and Hades.

34

But honors you; and every one doth wish
You had but that opinion of yourself
Which every noble Roman bears of you.
This is Trebonius.

BRUTUS

He is welcome hither.

CASSIUS

This, Decius Brutus.

BRUTUS

He is welcome too.

CASSIUS

This, Casca; this, Cinna; and this, Metellus
Cimber.

BRUTUS

They are all welcome.
What watchful cares do interpose themselves
Betwixt your eyes and night?

CASSIUS

Shall I entreat a word?   100

Cassius and Brutus whisper aside.

DECIUS

Here lies the east. Doth not the day break here?

CASCA

No.

CINNA

O pardon, sir, it doth; and yon gray lines
That fret [17] the clouds are messengers of day.

CASCA

You shall confess that you are both deceived.
Here, as I point my sword, the sun arises,
Which is a great way growing on the south,
Weighing the youthful season of the year.
Some two months hence, up higher toward the
    north
He first presents his fire, and the high east   **110**
Stands as the Capitol, directly here.

BRUTUS

Give me your hands all over, one by one.

CASSIUS

And let us swear our resolution.

BRUTUS

No, not an oath. If not the face of men,
The sufferance [18] of our souls, the time's abuse—
If these be motives weak, break off betimes,
And every man hence to his idle bed.
So let high-sighted [19] tyranny range on
Till each man drop by lottery. But if these—
As I am sure they do—bear fire enough   **120**
To kindle cowards and to steel with valor
The melting spirits of women, then, countrymen,
What need we any spur but our own cause

[17] interlace   [18] distress   [19] arrogant

To prick [20] us to redress? What other bond
Than secret Romans that have spoke the word
And will not palter? [21] And what other oath
Than honesty to honesty engaged,
That this shall be, or we will fall for it?
Swear priests and cowards and men cautelous,[22]
Old feeble carrions,[23] and such suffering souls   130
That welcome wrongs; unto bad causes swear
Such creatures as men doubt; but do not stain
The even virtue of our enterprise,
Nor the insuppressive [24] mettle of our spirits,
To think that or [25] our cause or our performance
Did need an oath; when every drop of blood
That every Roman bears, and nobly bears,
Is guilty of a several bastardy
If he do break the smallest particle
Of any promise that hath passed from him.   140

CASSIUS

But what of Cicero? Shall we sound him?
I think he will stand very strong with us.

CASCA

Let us not leave him out.

CINNA

        No, by no means.

METELLUS

O let us have him, for his silver hairs
Will purchase us a good opinion
And buy men's voices to commend our deeds.

---

[20] urge   [21] doubletalk   [22] deceitful   [23] corpses
[24] invincible   [25] either

It shall be said his judgment ruled our hands;
Our youths and wildness shall no whit [26] appear,
But all be buried in his gravity.

BRUTUS

O name him not! Let us not break with [27] him;   150
For he will never follow anything
That other men begin.

CASSIUS

       Then leave him out.

CASCA

Indeed he is not fit.

DECIUS

Shall no man else be touched, but only Caesar?

CASSIUS

Decius, well urged. I think it is not meet
Mark Antony, so well beloved of Caesar,
Should outlive Caesar. We shall find of him
A shrewd contriver; and you know his means,
If he improve them, may well stretch so far
As to annoy us all; which to prevent,   160
Let Antony and Caesar fall together.

BRUTUS

Our course will seem too bloody, Caius Cassius,
To cut the head off and then hack the limbs,
Like wrath in death and envy afterwards;

26 *no whit:* not at all   27 *break with:* confide in

For Antony is but a limb of Caesar.
Let's be sacrificers, but not butchers, Caius.
We all stand up against the spirit of Caesar,
And in the spirit of men there is no blood.
O that we then could come by Caesar's spirit,
And not dismember Caesar! But, alas,   **170**
Caesar must bleed for it! And gentle friends,
Let's kill him boldly, but not wrathfully;
Let's carve him as a dish fit for the gods,
Not hew him as a carcass fit for hounds.
And let our hearts, as subtle masters do,
Stir up their servants to an act of rage
And after seem to chide 'em.[28] This shall make
Our purpose necessary and not envious;
Which so appearing to the common eyes,
We shall be called purgers, not murderers.   **180**
And for Mark Antony, think not of him;
For he can do no more than Caesar's arm
When Caesar's head is off.

CASSIUS

Yet I fear him,
For in the ingrafted love he bears to Caesar—

BRUTUS

Alas, good Cassius, do not think of him.
If he love Caesar, all that he can do
Is to himself—take thought, and die for Caesar;
And that were much he [29] should, for he is given
To sports, to wildness, and much company.

[28] *And let . . . chide 'em*: let our hearts provoke our
hands to do the evil deed, but then still feel guilty for it.
[29] *if he*

There is no fear in him. Let him not die;   **190**
For he will live, and laugh at this hereafter.

Clock strikes.[30]

BRUTUS

Peace, count the clock.

CASSIUS

The clock hath stricken three.

TREBONIUS

'Tis time to part.

CASSIUS

But it is doubtful yet
Whether Caesar will come forth today or no;
For he is superstitious grown of late,
Quite from the main opinion he held once
Of fantasy, of dreams, and ceremonies.
It may be these apparent prodigies,[31]
The unaccustomed terror of this night,
And the persuasion of his augurers,   **200**
May hold him from the Capitol today.

DECIUS

Never fear that. If he be so resolved,
I can o'ersway him; for he loves to hear
That unicorns may be betrayed with trees,
And bears with glasses, elephants with holes,
Lions with toils,[32] and men with flatterers;

[30] *Striking clocks, unknown to Caesar's time, were used in Elizabethan England.*   [31] bad omens   [32] nets

But when I tell him he hates flatterers,
He says he does, being then most flattered.
Let me work,
For I can give his humor the true bent,[33]   210
And I will bring him to the Capitol.

CASSIUS

Nay, we will all of us be there to fetch him.

BRUTUS

By the eighth hour. Is that the uttermost?[34]

CINNA

Be that the uttermost, and fail not then.

METELLUS

Caius Ligarius doth bear Caesar hard,
Who rated[35] him for speaking well of Pompey.
I wonder none of you have thought of him.

BRUTUS

Now, good Metellus, go along by[36] him.
He loves me well, and I have given him reasons.
Send him but hither, and I'll fashion[37] him.   220

CASSIUS

The morning comes upon 's. We'll leave you,
   Brutus.
And friends disperse yourselves, but all remem-
   ber
What you have said, and show yourselves true
   Romans.

[33] *give . . . bent:* influence his mood   [34] latest   [35] criticized
[36] *go along by:* call on   [37] influence

BRUTUS

Good gentlemen, look fresh and merrily.
Let not our looks put on [38] our purposes,
But bear it as our Roman actors do,
With untired spirits and formal constancy.
And so, good morrow to you every one.

Exeunt all but Brutus.

Boy! Lucius! Fast asleep? It is no matter.
Enjoy the honey-heavy dew of slumber.   230
Thou hast no figures [39] nor no fantasies
Which busy care draws in the brains of men;
Therefore thou sleepest so sound.

Enter Portia.

PORTIA

Brutus, my lord.

BRUTUS

Portia! What mean you? Wherefore rise you
now?
It is not for your health thus to commit
Your weak condition to the raw cold morning.

PORTIA

Nor for yours neither. You've ungently, Brutus,
Stole from my bed. And yesternight at supper
You suddenly arose and walked about,
Musing and sighing with your arms across; [40]   240
And when I asked you what the matter was,
You stared upon me with ungentle looks.

---

[38] *put on:* reveal   [39] dreams   [40] folded

I urged you further; then you scratched your
  head
And too impatiently stamped with your foot.
Yet I insisted; yet you answered not,
But with an angry wafture [41] of your hand
Gave sign for me to leave you. So I did,
Fearing to strengthen that impatience
Which seemed too much enkindled; and withal
Hoping it was but an effect of humor,[42]   250
Which sometime hath his hour with every man.
It will not let you eat, nor talk, nor sleep;
And could it work so much upon your shape
As it hath much prevailed on your condition,
I should not know you, Brutus. Dear my lord,
Make me acquainted with your cause of grief.

BRUTUS

I am not well in health, and that is all.

PORTIA

Brutus is wise, and were he not in health,
He would embrace the means to come by it.

BRUTUS

Why, so I do. Good Portia, go to bed.   260

PORTIA

Is Brutus sick, and is it physical [43]
To walk unbraced and suck up the humors
Of the dank morning? What, is Brutus sick,
And will he steal out of his wholesome bed
To dare the vile contagion of the night,
And tempt the rheumy [44] and unpurged air,

[41] wave   [42] mood   [43] healthful   [44] damp

43

To add unto his sickness? No, my Brutus,
You have some sick offense within your mind,
Which by the right and virtue of my place
I ought to know of. And upon my knees   270
I charm you, by my once commended beauty,
By all your vows of love, and that great vow
Which did incorporate [45] and make us one,
That you unfold to me your self, your half,
Why you are heavy,[46] and what men tonight
Have had resort to you; for here have been
Some six or seven who did hide their faces
Even from darkness.

BRUTUS

        Kneel not, gentle Portia.

PORTIA

I should not need, if you were gentle Brutus.
Within the bond of marriage, tell me, Brutus,   280
Is it excepted I should know no secrets
That appertain to you? Am I your self
But, as it were, in sort or limitation?
To keep with you at meals, comfort your bed,
And talk to you sometimes? Dwell I but in the
    suburbs
Of your good pleasure? If it be no more,
Portia is Brutus' harlot, not his wife.

BRUTUS

You are my true and honorable wife,
As dear to me as are the ruddy [47] drops

[45] unite   [46] pensive   [47] red

That visit my sad heart.

PORTIA

If this were true, then should I know this secret.
I grant I am a woman; but withal,
A woman that Lord Brutus took to wife.
I grant I am a woman; but withal,
A woman well reputed—Cato's [48] daughter.
Think you I am no stronger than my sex,
Being so fathered and so husbanded?
Tell me your counsels; I will not disclose 'em.
I have made strong proof of my constancy,
Giving myself a voluntary wound   300
Here, in the thigh. Can I bear that with patience,
And not my husband's secrets?

BRUTUS

                    O ye gods,
Render me worthy of this noble wife!   *Knock.*
Hark, hark, one knocks. Portia, go in awhile,
And by and by thy bosom shall partake
The secrets of my heart.
All my engagement I will construe [49] to thee,
All the charactery [50] of my sad brows.
Leave me with haste.   *Exit Portia.*

        Enter Lucius and Ligarius.

                    Lucius, who's that knocks?

LUCIUS

Here is a sick man that would speak with you.   310

---

[48] *Marcus Cato, Portia's father, was a friend of Pompey. He committed suicide after Caesar defeated Pompey.* [49] describe [50] expression

BRUTUS

Caius Ligarius, that Metellus spake of.
Boy, stand aside. Caius Ligarius, how?

LIGARIUS

Vouchsafe good morrow from a feeble tongue.

BRUTUS

O what a time have you chose out, brave Caius,
To wear a kerchief! [51] Would you were not sick.

LIGARIUS

I am not sick, if Brutus have in hand
Any exploit worthy the name of honor.

BRUTUS

Such an exploit have I in hand, Ligarius,
Had you a healthful ear to hear of it.

LIGARIUS

By all the gods that Romans bow before,   320
I here discard my sickness! Soul of Rome!
Brave son, derived from honorable loins!
Thou like an exorcist hast conjured up
My mortified spirit. Now bid me run,
And I will strive with things impossible—
Yea, get the better of them. What's to do?

BRUTUS

A piece of work that will make sick men whole.

LIGARIUS

But are not some whole that we must make sick?

[51] *Romans wore kerchiefs to show they were ill.*

BRUTUS

That must we also. What it is, my Caius,
I shall unfold to thee as we are going   **330**
To whom it must be done.

LIGARIUS

                    Set on your foot,
And with a heart new-fired I follow you,
To do I know not what; but it sufficeth
That Brutus leads me on.

BRUTUS

                    Follow me then. *Exeunt.*

ACT TWO, SCENE TWO

*Rome. Caesar's house. Thunder and
lightning. Enter Caesar in his nightgown.*

CAESAR

Nor heaven nor earth have been at peace tonight.
Thrice hath Calpurnia in her sleep cried out
"Help ho, they murder Caesar!" Who's within?

Enter Servant.

SERVANT

My lord?

CAESAR

Go bid the priests do present sacrifice,
And bring me their opinions of success.

SERVANT

I will, my lord.   *Exit.*

47

Enter Calpurnia.

CALPURNIA

What mean you, Caesar? Think you to walk
forth?
You shall not stir out of your house today.

CAESAR

Caesar shall forth. The things that threatened me   10
Ne'er looked but on my back. When they shall
see
The face of Caesar, they are vanished.

CALPURNIA

Caesar, I never stood on ceremonies,[1]
Yet now they fright me. There is one within,
Besides the things that we have heard and seen,
Recounts most horrid sights seen by the watch.
A lioness hath whelped in the streets;
And graves have yawned and yielded up their
dead;
Fierce fiery warriors fought upon the clouds
In ranks and squadrons and right form [2] of war,   20
Which drizzled blood upon the Capitol.
The noise of battle hurtled in the air;
Horses did neigh, and dying men did groan,
And ghosts did shriek and squeal about the
streets.
O Caesar, these things are beyond all use,[3]
And I do fear them.

CAESAR

What can be avoided

[1] *stood on ceremonies*: believed omens   [2] correct order
[3] experience

48

Whose end is purposed by the mighty gods?
Yet Caesar shall go forth, for these predictions
Are to the world in general as to Caesar.

CALPURNIA

When beggars die, there are no comets seen; 30
The heavens themselves blaze forth the death of
  princes.

CAESAR

Cowards die many times before their deaths;
The valiant never taste of death but once.
Of all the wonders that I yet have heard,
It seems to me most strange that men should fear,
Seeing that death, a necessary end,
Will come when it will come.

Enter Servant.

What say the augurers?

SERVANT

They would not have you to stir forth today.
Plucking the entrails of an offering forth,
They could not find a heart within the beast. 40

CAESAR

The gods do this in shame of cowardice.
Caesar should be a beast without a heart
If he should stay at home today for fear.
No, Caesar shall not. Danger knows full well
That Caesar is more dangerous than he.
We were two lions littered in one day,
And I the elder and more terrible;
And Caesar shall go forth.

49

CALPURNIA

　　　　　　Alas, my lord,
Your wisdom is consumed in confidence.
Do not go forth today. Call it my fear   **50**
That keeps you in the house, and not your own.
We'll send Mark Antony to the Senate House,
And he shall say you are not well today.
Let me upon my knee prevail in this.

CAESAR

Mark Antony shall say I am not well,
And for thy humor I will stay at home.

Enter Decius.

Here's Decius Brutus; he shall tell them so.

DECIUS

Caesar, all hail! Good morrow, worthy Caesar!
I come to fetch you to the Senate House.

CAESAR

And you are come in very happy time   **60**
To bear my greetings to the senators,
And tell them that I will not come today.
Cannot, is false; and that I dare not, falser.
I will not come today; tell them so, Decius.

CALPURNIA

Say he is sick.

CAESAR

　　　　Shall Caesar send a lie?
Have I in conquest stretched mine arm so far

50

To be afeared to tell greybeards the truth?
Decius, go tell them: Caesar will not come.

DECIUS

Most mighty Caesar, let me know some cause,
Lest I be laughed at when I tell them so.   70

CAESAR

The cause is in my will; I will not come.
That is enough to satisfy the senate.
But for your private satisfaction,
Because I love you, I will let you know.
Calpurnia here, my wife, stays me at home.
She dreamt tonight she saw my statue,
Which, like a fountain with an hundred spouts,
Did run pure blood; and many lusty Romans
Came smiling and did bathe their hands in it.
And these does she apply for warnings and por-
    tents   80
And evils imminent; and on her knee
Hath begged that I will stay at home today.

DECIUS

This dream is all amiss interpreted;
It was a vision fair and fortunate.
Your statue spouting blood in many pipes,
In which so many smiling Romans bathed,
Signifies that from you great Rome shall suck
Reviving blood, and that great men shall press
For tinctures, stains, relics, and cognizance.
This by Calpurnia's dream is signified.   90

CAESAR

And this way have you well expounded it.

51

DECIUS

I have, when you have heard what I can say;
And know it now—the Senate have concluded
To give this day a crown to mighty Caesar.
If you shall send them word you will not come,
Their minds may change. Besides, it were a mock
Apt to be rendered [4] for some one to say
"Break up the Senate till another time,
When Caesar's wife shall meet with better
    dreams."
If Caesar hide himself, shall they not whisper   100
"Lo, Caesar is afraid"?
Pardon me Caesar, for my dear dear love
To your proceeding [5] bids me tell you this;
And reason to my love is liable.

CAESAR

How foolish do your fears seem now, Calpurnia!
I am ashamed I did yield to them.
Give me my robe, for I will go.

*Enter Brutus, Ligarius, Metellus, Casca,
    Trebonius, Cinna, and Publius.*

And look where Publius is come to fetch me.

PUBLIUS

Good morrow, Caesar.

CAESAR

                    Welcome, Publius.
What, Brutus, are you stirred so early too?   110

4 *mock . . . rendered*: criticism apt to be made
5 advancement

Good morrow, Casca. Caius Ligarius,
Caesar was ne'er so much your enemy
As that same ague [6] which hath made you lean.
What is't o'clock?

BRUTUS

Caesar, 'tis strucken eight.

CAESAR

I thank you for your pains and courtesy.

Enter Antony.

See, Antony that revels long o'nights
Is notwithstanding up. Good morrow, Antony.

ANTONY

So to most noble Caesar.

CAESAR

Bid them prepare within;
I am to blame to be thus waited for.
Now, Cinna. Now, Metellus. What, Trebonius,   120
I have an hour's talk in store for you;
Remember that you call on me today.
Be near me, that I may remember you.

TREBONIUS

Caesar, I will. *[aside]* And so near will I be,
That your best friends shall wish I had been
    further.

CAESAR

Good friends, go in and taste some wine with me,

6 illness

And we, like friends, will straightway go
  together.

BRUTUS [aside]

That every like is not the same, O Caesar,
The heart of Brutus yearns to think upon.

Exeunt.

ACT TWO, SCENE THREE

*Rome. Before Caesar's house.
Enter Artemidorus with a paper.*

ARTEMIDORUS [reads]

*Caesar, beware of Brutus; take heed of Cassius;
come not near Casca; have an eye to Cinna; trust
not Trebonius; mark well Metellus Cimber; Decius Brutus loves thee not; thou hast wronged
Caius Ligarius. There is but one mind in all these
men, and it is bent against Caesar. If thou beest
not immortal, look about you. Security gives way
to conspiracy. The mighty gods defend thee.*
                        Thy lover,[1] Artemidorus.

Here will I stand till Caesar pass along,   10
And as a suitor [2] will I give him this.
My heart laments that virtue cannot live
Out of the teeth of emulation.[3]
If thou read this, O Caesar, thou mayest live;
If not, the Fates with traitors do contrive.

Exit.

[1] friend   [2] petitioner   [3] rivalry

ACT TWO, SCENE FOUR

Rome. Before Brutus' house.
Enter Portia and Lucius.

PORTIA

I prithee, boy, run to the Senate House;
Stay not to answer me, but get thee gone.
Why dost thou stay?

LUCIUS

     To know my errand, madam.

PORTIA

I would have had thee there and here again,
Ere I can tell thee what thou shouldst do there.
[aside] O constancy, be strong upon my side.
Set a huge mountain 'tween my heart and tongue!
I have a man's mind, but a woman's might.
How hard it is for women to keep counsel!
Art thou here yet?

LUCIUS

    Madam, what should I do?   **10**
Run to the Capitol, and nothing else?
And so return to you, and nothing else?

PORTIA

Yes, bring me word, boy, if thy lord look well,
For he went sickly forth; and take good note
What Caesar doth, what suitors press to him.
Hark, boy! What noise is that?

LUCIUS

I hear none, madam.

PORTIA

Prithee, listen well.
I heard a bustling rumor [1] like a fray,
And the wind brings it from the Capitol.

LUCIUS

Sooth, madam, I hear nothing.   20

Enter Soothsayer.

PORTIA

Come hither, fellow. Which way hast thou been?

SOOTHSAYER

At mine own house, good lady.

PORTIA

What is't o'clock?

SOOTHSAYER

About the ninth hour, lady.

PORTIA

Is Caesar yet gone to the Capitol?

SOOTHSAYER

Madam, not yet. I go to take my stand
To see him pass on to the Capitol.

[1] hubbub

PORTIA

Thou hast some suit to Caesar, hast thou not?

SOOTHSAYER

That I have, lady. If it will please Caesar
To be so good to Caesar as to hear me,
I shall beseech him to befriend himself. 30

PORTIA

Why, knowest thou any harm's intended towards
him?

SOOTHSAYER

None that I know will be, much that I fear may
chance.[2]
Good morrow to you. Here the street is narrow.
The throng that follows Caesar at the heels,
Of senators, of praetors, common suitors,
Will crowd a feeble man almost to death.
I'll get me to a place more void,[3] and there
Speak to great Caesar as he comes along. *Exit.*

PORTIA

I must go in. Ay me! How weak a thing
The heart of woman is! O Brutus, 40
The heavens speed thee in thine enterprise.—
Sure the boy heard me.—Brutus hath a suit
That Caesar will not grant.—O, I grow faint.—
Run, Lucius, and commend me to my lord;
Say I am merry. Come to me again,
And bring me word what he doth say to thee.

Exeunt separately.

[2] happen   [3] empty

ACT THREE, SCENE ONE

*Rome. Before the Capitol. Enter Citizens,
Artemidorus, and Soothsayer. Flourish.
Enter Caesar, Brutus, Cassius, Casca,
Decius, Metellus, Trebonius, Cinna,
Antony, Lepidus, Popilius, and Publius.*

CAESAR

The ides of March are come.

SOOTHSAYER

Ay, Caesar, but not gone.

ARTEMIDORUS

Hail, Caesar! Read this schedule.[1]

DECIUS

Trebonius doth desire you to o'er-read
At your best leisure this his humble suit.

ARTEMIDORUS

O Caesar, read mine first; for mine's a suit
That touches Caesar nearer. Read it, great
    Caesar.

CAESAR

What touches us ourself shall be last served.

ARTEMIDORUS

Delay not, Caesar! Read it instantly.

[1] petition

CAESAR

What, is the fellow mad?

PUBLIUS

        Sirrah, give place.   **10**

CASSIUS

What, urge you your petitions in the street?
Come to the Capitol.

POPILIUS

I wish your enterprise today may thrive.

CASSIUS

What enterprise, Popilius?

POPILIUS

        Fare you well.

BRUTUS

What said Popilius Lena?

CASSIUS

He wished today our enterprise might thrive.
I fear our purpose is discovered.

BRUTUS

Look how he makes to [2] Caesar. Mark him.

CASSIUS

Casca, be sudden, for we fear prevention.
Brutus, what shall be done? If this be known,   **20**

2 *makes to:* moves toward

Cassius or Caesar never shall turn back,
For I will slay myself.

BRUTUS

Cassius, be constant.[3]
Popilius Lena speaks not of our purposes,
For look he smiles, and Caesar doth not change.

CASSIUS

Trebonius knows his time, for look you, Brutus,
He draws Mark Antony out of the way.

Exeunt Antony and Trebonius.

DECIUS

Where is Metellus Cimber? Let him go,
And presently prefer [4] his suit to Caesar.

BRUTUS

He is addressed; press near and second him.

CINNA

Casca, you are the first that rears your hand.   30

CAESAR

Are we all ready? What is now amiss
That Caesar and his senate must redress?

METELLUS

Most high, most mighty, and most puissant [5]
    Caesar,
Metellus Cimber throws before thy seat
An humble heart.

[3] steady   [4] present   [5] powerful

CAESAR

              I must prevent thee, Cimber.
These couchings [6] and these lowly courtesies
Might fire the blood of ordinary men
And turn pre-ordinance and first decree
Into the law of children. Be not fond,[7]
To think that Caesar bears such rebel blood   **40**
That will be thawed from the true quality
With that which melteth fools; I mean sweet
   words,
Low-crooked curtsies, and base spaniel fawning.
Thy brother by decree is banished.
If thou dost bend, and pray, and fawn for him,
I spurn thee like a cur out of my way.
Know, Caesar doth not wrong, nor without cause
Will he be satisfied.

METELLUS

Is there no voice more worthy than my own,
To sound more sweetly in great Caesar's ear   **50**
For the repealing [8] of my banished brother?

BRUTUS

I kiss thy hand, but not in flattery, Caesar;
Desiring thee that Publius Cimber may
Have an immediate freedom of repeal.

CAESAR

What, Brutus?

CASSIUS

            Pardon, Caesar; Caesar, pardon.

[6] bowings   [7] *Be not fond*: Be not so foolish   [8] return

As low as to thy foot doth Cassius fall,
To beg enfranchisement for Publius Cimber.

CAESAR

I could be well moved, if I were as you;
If I could pray to move,⁹ prayers would move me.
But I am constant as the northern star, **60**
Of whose true-fixed and resting quality
There is no fellow in the firmament.
The skies are painted with unnumbered sparks,
They are all fire, and every one doth shine;
But there's but one in all doth hold his place.
So in the world; 'tis furnished well with men,
And men are flesh and blood, and apprehensive;
Yet in the number I do know but one
That unassailable holds on his rank,
Unshaked of motion: and that I am he. **70**
Let me a little show it, even in this—
That I was constant Cimber should be banished,
And constant do remain to keep him so.

CINNA

O Caesar—

CAESAR

Hence! Wilt thou lift up Olympus?

DECIUS

Great Caesar—

CAESAR

Doth not Brutus bootless ¹⁰ kneel?

⁹ *pray to move*: beg a favor   ¹⁰ vainly

CASCA

Speak, hands, for me.

> *They stab Caesar, Casca first,*
> *Brutus last.*

CAESAR

Et tu, Bruté? Then fall Caesar.   *Dies.*

CINNA

Liberty! Freedom! Tyranny is dead!
Run hence, proclaim, cry it about the streets.

CASSIUS

Some to the common pulpits,[11] and cry out   80
"Liberty, freedom, and enfranchisement!"

BRUTUS

People and senators, be not affrighted.
Fly not, stand still. Ambition's debt is paid.

CASCA

Go to the pulpit, Brutus.

DECIUS

> And Cassius too.

BRUTUS

Where's Publius?

CINNA

Here, quite confounded with this mutiny.

[11] speaker's platforms

63

METELLUS

Stand fast together, lest some friend of Caesar's
Should chance—

BRUTUS

Talk not of standing. Publius, good cheer,
There is no harm intended to your person,   90
Nor to no Roman else: so tell them, Publius.

CASSIUS

And leave us, Publius, lest that the people
Rushing on us should do your age some mischief.

BRUTUS

Do so; and let no man abide [12] this deed
But we the doers.

Enter Trebonius.

CASSIUS

Where is Antony?

TREBONIUS

       Fled to his house amazed.
Men, wives, and children stare, cry out, and run
As it were doomsday.

BRUTUS

       Fates, we will know your pleasures.
That we shall die we know; 'tis but the time,
And drawing days out, that men stand upon. [13]   100

CASCA

Why, he that cuts off twenty years of life

[12] pay for   [13] *stand upon:* live for

Cuts off so many years of fearing death.

Grant that, and then is death a benefit;
So are we Caesar's friends, that have abridged
His time of fearing death. Stoop, Romans, stoop,
And let us bathe our hands in Caesar's blood
Up to the elbows, and besmear our swords;
Then walk we forth even to the market place,
And waving our red weapons o'er our heads,
Let's all cry "Peace, freedom, and liberty!"   110

Stoop then and wash. How many ages hence
Shall this our lofty scene be acted over
In states unborn and accents yet unknown!

How many times shall Caesar bleed in sport,
That now on Pompey's basis [14] lies along
No worthier than the dust.

                    So oft as that shall be,
So often shall the knot [15] of us be called
The men that gave their country liberty.

What, shall we forth?

                    Ay, every man away.
Brutus shall lead, and we will grace his heels   120

14 base of statue   15 band

65

With the most boldest and best hearts of Rome.

Enter Servant.

BRUTUS

Soft, who comes here? A friend of Antony's.

SERVANT

Thus, Brutus, did my master bid me kneel;
Thus did Mark Antony bid me fall down,
And being prostrate, thus he bade me say:
Brutus is noble, wise, valiant, and honest;
Caesar was mighty, bold, royal, and loving.
Say I love Brutus, and I honor him;
Say I feared Caesar, honored him, and loved him.
If Brutus will vouchsafe [16] that Antony   130
May safely come to him, and be resolved
How Caesar hath deserved to lie in death,
Mark Antony shall not love Caesar dead
So well as Brutus living; but will follow
The fortunes and affairs of noble Brutus
Through the hazards of this untrod [17] state
With all true faith. So says my master Antony.

BRUTUS

Thy master is a wise and valiant Roman;
I never thought him worse.
Tell him, so please him come unto this place,   140
He shall be satisfied and, by my honor,
Depart untouched.

SERVANT

I'll fetch him presently.[18]
Exit.

[16] allow   [17] new   [18] now

66

BRUTUS

I know that we shall have him well to friend.

CASSIUS

I wish we may. But yet have I a mind
That fears him much; and my misgiving still
Falls shrewdly to the purpose.

Enter Antony.

BRUTUS

But here comes Antony. Welcome, Mark Antony.

ANTONY

O mighty Caesar! Dost thou lie so low?
Are all thy conquests, glories, triumphs, spoils,
Shrunk to this little measure? Fare thee well.   150
I know not, gentlemen, what you intend,
Who else must be let blood, who else is rank:[19]
If I myself, there is no hour so fit
As Caesar's death's hour; nor no instrument
Of half that worth as those your swords, made
    rich
With the most noble blood of all this world.
I do beseech ye, if you bear me hard,
Now, whilst your purpled hands do reek and
    smoke,
Fulfill your pleasure. Live a thousand years,
I shall not find myself so apt to die.   160
No place will please me so, no mean [20] of death,
As here by Caesar, and by you cut off,
The choice and master spirits of this age.

[19] diseased   [20] manner

BRUTUS

O Antony, beg not your death of us!
Though now we must appear bloody and cruel,
As by our hands, and this our present act,
You see we do; yet see you but our hands,
And this the bleeding business they have done.
Our hearts you see not. They are pitiful.
And pity to the general wrong of Rome—   170
As fire drives out fire, so pity pity—
Hath done this deed on Caesar. For your part,
To you our swords have leaden points, Mark
   Antony;
Our arms in strength of malice, and our hearts
Of brothers' temper, do receive you in
With all kind love, good thoughts, and reverence.

CASSIUS

Your voice shall be as strong as any man's
In the disposing of new dignities.

BRUTUS

Only be patient, till we have appeased
The multitude, beside themselves with fear,   180
And then we will deliver you the cause
Why I, that did love Caesar when I struck him,
Have thus proceeded.

ANTONY

           I doubt not of your wisdom.
Let each man render me his bloody hand.
First, Marcus Brutus, will I shake with you;
Next, Caius Cassius, do I take your hand;
Now, Decius Brutus, yours; now yours, Metellus;
Yours, Cinna; and my valiant Casca, yours;

Though last, not least in love, yours, good
    Trebonius.
Gentlemen all—alas, what shall I say?   190
My credit now stands on such slippery ground,
That one of two bad ways you must conceit [21]
    me,
Either a coward or a flatterer.
That I did love thee, Caesar, O 'tis true.
If then thy spirit look upon us now,
Shall it not grieve thee dearer than thy death
To see thy Antony making his peace,
Shaking the bloody fingers of thy foes,
Most noble, in the presence of thy corse? [22]
Had I as many eyes as thou hast wounds,   200
Weeping as fast as they stream forth thy blood,
It would become me better than to close
In terms of friendship with thine enemies.
Pardon me, Julius! Here wast thou bayed, brave
    hart,[23]
Here didst thou fall; and here thy hunters stand,
Signed in thy spoil and crimsoned in thy lethe.[24]
O world, thou wast the forest to this hart,
And this indeed, O world, the heart of thee.
How like a deer, strucken by many princes,
Dost thou here lie.   210

CASSIUS

Mark Antony—

ANTONY

            Pardon me, Caius Cassius.
The enemies of Caesar shall say this;
Then, in a friend, it is cold modesty.[25]

[21] judge   [22] corpse   [23] stag   [24] blood   [25] moderation

CASSIUS

I blame you not for praising Caesar so,
But what compact mean you to have with us?
Will you be pricked [26] in number of our friends,
Or shall we on, and not depend on you?

ANTONY

Therefore I took your hand, but was indeed
Swayed from the point by looking down on
    Caesar.
Friends am I with you all, and love you all   **220**
Upon this hope, that you shall give me reasons
Why and wherein Caesar was dangerous.

BRUTUS

Or else were this a savage spectacle.
Our reasons are so full of good regard,
That were you, Antony, the son of Caesar,
You should be satisfied.

ANTONY

           That's all I seek;
And am moreover suitor that I may
Produce his body to the market place;
And in the pulpit, as becomes a friend,
Speak in the order of his funeral.   **230**

BRUTUS

You shall, Mark Antony.

CASSIUS

           Brutus, a word with you.

[26] marked, included

[aside to Brutus.]
You know not what you do. Do not consent
That Antony speak in his funeral.
Know you how much the people may be moved
By that which he will utter?

BRUTUS   *[aside to Cassius]*

By your pardon.
I will myself into the pulpit first,
And show the reason of our Caesar's death.
What Antony shall speak, I will protest
He speaks by leave and by permission;
And that we are contented Caesar shall   240
Have all true rites and lawful ceremonies.
It shall advantage more than do us wrong.

CASSIUS *[aside to Brutus]*

I know not what may fall.[27] I like it not.

BRUTUS

Mark Antony, here take you Caesar's body.
You shall not in your funeral speech blame us,
But speak all good you can devise of Caesar,
And say you do't by our permission;
Else shall you not have any hand at all
About his funeral. And you shall speak
In the same pulpit whereto I am going,   250
After my speech is ended.

ANTONY

Be it so.
I do desire no more.

[27] happen

71

Prepare the body then, and follow us.

Exeunt all but Antony.

ANTONY

O pardon me, thou bleeding piece of earth,
That I am meek and gentle with these butchers.
Thou art the ruins of the noblest man
That ever lived in the tide of times.
Woe to the hand that shed this costly blood!
Over thy wounds now do I prophesy—
Which like dumb mouths do ope their ruby lips,   260
To beg the voice and utterance of my tongue—
A curse shall light upon the limbs of men;
Domestic fury and fierce civil strife
Shall cumber [28] all the parts of Italy.
Blood and destruction shall be so in use
And dreadful objects so familiar
That mothers shall but smile when they behold
Their infants quartered with the hands of war,
All pity choked with custom of fell deeds.[29]
And Caesar's spirit, ranging for revenge,   270
With Até [30] by his side come hot from hell,
Shall in these confines with a monarch's voice
Cry "Havoc," [31] and let slip the dogs of war,
That this foul deed shall smell above the earth
With carrion men, groaning for burial.

Enter Octavius' Servant.

You serve Octavius Caesar, do you not?

---

28 burden   29 *All . . . deeds:* people will be so used to cruelty, they no longer will feel pity.   30 *Até, Greek goddess of discord and destruction, lived in Hades.*

31 *"Havoc" was a battlecry, signifying total slaughter.*

SERVANT

I do, Mark Antony.

ANTONY

Caesar did write for him to come to Rome.

SERVANT

He did receive his letters and is coming,
And bid me say to you by word of mouth—   280
O Caesar!

ANTONY

Thy heart is big. Get thee apart and weep.
Passion, I see, is catching, for mine eyes,
Seeing those beads of sorrow stand in thine,
Began to water. Is thy master coming?

SERVANT

He lies tonight within seven leagues of Rome.

ANTONY

Post back with speed, and tell him what hath
   chanced.[32]
Here is a mourning Rome, a dangerous Rome,
No Rome of safety for Octavius yet.
Hie hence, and tell him so. Yet stay awhile;   290
Thou shalt not back till I have borne this corse
Into the market place. There shall I try [33]
In my oration, how the people take
The cruel issue [34] of these bloody men;
According to the which, thou shalt discourse
To young Octavius of the state of things.
Lend me your hand.

                  Exeunt with Caesar's body.

[32] happened   [33] test   [34] deed

ACT THREE, SCENE TWO

Rome. The Forum. Enter Brutus and Cassius, with the Citizens.

CITIZENS

We will be satisfied! Let us be satisfied!

BRUTUS

Then follow me and give me audience, friends.
Cassius, go you into the other street
And part [1] the numbers.
Those that will hear me speak, let 'em stay here;
Those that will follow Cassius, go with him;
And public reasons shall be rendered
Of Caesar's death.

FIRST CITIZEN

    I will hear Brutus speak.

SECOND CITIZEN

I will hear Cassius, and compare their reasons
When severally [2] we hear them rendered.   **10**

Exit Cassius, with some Citizens. Brutus goes into the pulpit.

THIRD CITIZEN

The noble Brutus is ascended! Silence!

BRUTUS

Be patient till the last.

[1] divide   [2] separately

Romans, countrymen, and lovers,[3] hear me for my cause, and be silent, that you may hear. Believe me for mine honor, and have respect to mine honor, that you may believe. Censure [4] me in your wisdom, and awake your senses, that you may the better judge. If there be any in this assembly, any dear friend of Caesar's, to him I say that Brutus' love to Caesar was no less than his. If then that friend demand [5] why Brutus rose against Caesar, this is my answer: not that I loved Caesar less but that I loved Rome more. Had you rather Caesar were living, and die all slaves, than that Caesar were dead, to live all free men? As Caesar loved me, I weep for him; as he was fortunate, I rejoice at it; as he was valiant, I honor him: but as he was ambitious, I slew him. There is tears for his love; joy for his fortune; honor for his valor; and death for his ambition. Who is here so base that would be a bondman? [6] If any, speak, for him have I offended. Who is here so rude [7] that would not be a Roman? If any, speak, for him have I offended. Who is here so vile that will not love his country? If any, speak, for him have I offended. I pause for a reply.

CITIZENS

None, Brutus, none.

BRUTUS

Then none have I offended. I have done no more to Caesar than you shall do to Brutus. The question of his death is enrolled [8] in the Capitol; his

---

[3] friends   [4] judge   [5] ask   [6] slave   [7] barbarous   [8] recorded

glory not extenuated,[9] wherein he was worthy; nor his offenses enforced,[10] for which he suffered death.

Enter Antony with Caesar's body.

Here comes his body, mourned by Mark Antony, who though he had no hand in his death, shall receive the benefit of his dying, a place in the commonwealth, as which of you shall not? With this I depart,—that as I slew my best lover for the good of Rome, I have the same dagger for myself, when it shall please my country to need my death.

50

CITIZENS

Live Brutus! Live, live!

FIRST CITIZEN

Bring him with triumph home unto his house.

SECOND CITIZEN

Give him a statue with his ancestors.

THIRD CITIZEN

Let him be Caesar.

FOURTH CITIZEN

Caesar's better parts [11]
Shall be crowned in Brutus.

FIRST CITIZEN

We'll bring him to his house with shouts and clamors.

[9] understated   [10] exaggerated   [11] qualities

BRUTUS

My countrymen—

SECOND CITIZEN

Peace! Silence! Brutus speaks.

FIRST CITIZEN

Peace ho!

BRUTUS

Good countrymen, let me depart alone,
And for my sake, stay here with Antony.
Do grace to Caesar's corpse, and grace his speech
Tending to Caesar's glories, which Mark Antony
By our permission is allowed to make.
I do entreat you, not a man depart,
Save I alone, till Antony have spoke. *Exit.*

FIRST CITIZEN

Stay ho, and let us hear Mark Antony.

THIRD CITIZEN

Let him go up into the public chair,
We'll hear him. Noble Antony, go up.

ANTONY

For Brutus' sake, I am beholding to you.

Goes up to the pulpit.

FOURTH CITIZEN

What does he say of Brutus?

THIRD CITIZEN

He says for Brutus' sake

He finds himself beholding to us all.

FOURTH CITIZEN

'Twere best he speak no harm of Brutus here.

FIRST CITIZEN

This Caesar was a tyrant.

THIRD CITIZEN

Nay, that's certain.
We are blest that Rome is rid of him.

SECOND CITIZEN

Peace, let us hear what Antony can say.

ANTONY

You gentle Romans—

CITIZENS

Peace ho, let us hear him.

ANTONY

Friends, Romans, countrymen, lend me your ears.
I come to bury Caesar, not to praise him.   80
The evil that men do lives after them,
The good is oft interred with their bones;
So let it be with Caesar. The noble Brutus
Hath told you Caesar was ambitious;
If it were so, it was a grievous fault,
And grievously hath Caesar answered it.
Here, under leave of Brutus and the rest—
For Brutus is an honorable man,
So are they all, all honorable men—
Come I to speak in Caesar's funeral.   90

He was my friend, faithful and just to me;
But Brutus says he was ambitious,
And Brutus is an honorable man.
He hath brought many captives home to Rome,
Whose ransoms did the general coffers fill.
Did this in Caesar seem ambitious?
When that the poor have cried, Caesar hath wept.
Ambition should be made of sterner stuff;
Yet Brutus says he was ambitious,
And Brutus is an honorable man. 100
You all did see that on the Lupercal
I thrice presented him a kingly crown,
Which he did thrice refuse. Was this ambition?
Yet Brutus says he was ambitious,
And sure he is an honorable man.
I speak not to disprove what Brutus spoke,
But here I am to speak what I do know.
You all did love him once, not without cause;
What cause withholds you then to mourn for
    him?
O judgment, thou art fled to brutish beasts, 110
And men have lost their reason. Bear with me;
My heart is in the coffin there with Caesar,
And I must pause till it come back to me.

FIRST CITIZEN

Methinks there is much reason in his sayings.

SECOND CITIZEN

If thou consider rightly of the matter,
Caesar has had great wrong.

THIRD CITIZEN

                    Has he, masters?
I fear there will a worse come in his place.

FOURTH CITIZEN

Marked ye his words: He would not take the
  crown;
Therefore 'tis certain he was not ambitious.

FIRST CITIZEN

If it be found so, some will dear abide it.   **120**

SECOND CITIZEN

Poor soul, his eyes are red as fire with weeping.

THIRD CITIZEN

There's not a nobler man in Rome than Antony.

FOURTH CITIZEN

Now mark him, he begins again to speak.

ANTONY

But yesterday the word of Caesar might
Have stood against the world. Now lies he there,
And none so poor to do him reverence.
O masters, if I were disposed to stir
Your hearts and minds to mutiny and rage,
I should do Brutus wrong, and Cassius wrong,
Who you all know are honorable men.   **130**
I will not do them wrong. I rather choose
To wrong the dead, to wrong myself and you,
Than I will wrong such honorable men.
But here's a parchment with the seal of Caesar;
I found it in his closet,[12]—'tis his will.
Let but the commons [13] hear this testament—
Which, pardon me, I do not mean to read—

12 study   13 common people

And they would go and kiss dead Caesar's
  wounds,
And dip their napkins [14] in his sacred blood;   140
Yea, beg a hair of him for memory,
And dying, mention it within their wills,
Bequeathing it as a rich legacy
Unto their issue.

FOURTH CITIZEN

We'll hear the will. Read it, Mark Antony.

CITIZENS

The will, the will! We will hear Caesar's will.

ANTONY

Have patience, gentle friends. I must not read it.
It is not meet [15] you know how Caesar loved you.
You are not wood, you are not stones, but men;
And being men, hearing the will of Caesar,
It will inflame you, it will make you mad.   150
'Tis good you know not that you are his heirs,
For if you should, O what would come of it?

FOURTH CITIZEN

Read the will! We'll hear it, Antony!
You shall read us the will, Caesar's will.

ANTONY

Will you be patient? Will you stay awhile?
I have o'ershot myself to tell you of it.
I fear I wrong the honorable men
Whose daggers have stabbed Caesar; I do fear it.

[14] handkerchiefs   [15] fitting

FOURTH CITIZEN

They were traitors. Honorable men!

CITIZENS

The will! The testament! 160

SECOND CITIZEN

They were villains, murderers! The will! Read the
will!

ANTONY

You will compel me then to read the will?
Then make a ring about the corpse of Caesar,
And let me show you him that made the will.
Shall I descend? And will you give me leave? [16]

CITIZENS

Come down.

SECOND CITIZEN

Descend.

THIRD CITIZEN

You shall have leave. *Antony comes down.*

FOURTH CITIZEN

A ring, stand round.

FIRST CITIZEN

Stand from the hearse, stand from the body. 170

SECOND CITIZEN

Room for Antony, most noble Antony.

[16] permission

ANTONY

Nay, press not so upon me. Stand far off.

CITIZENS

Stand back. Room. Bear back.

ANTONY

If you have tears, prepare to shed them now.
You all do know this mantle.[17] I remember
The first time ever Caesar put it on—
'Twas on a summer's evening in his tent,
That day he overcame the Nervii.[18]
Look, in this place ran Cassius' dagger through.
See what a rent [19] the envious Casca made.   180
Through this the well-beloved Brutus stabbed;
And as he plucked his cursed steel away,
Mark how the blood of Caesar followed it,
As rushing out of doors, to be resolved
If Brutus so unkindly [20] knocked, or no;
For Brutus, as you know, was Caesar's angel.
Judge, O you gods, how dearly Caesar loved him.
This was the most unkindest cut of all,
For when the noble Caesar saw him stab,
Ingratitude, more strong than traitors' arms,   190
Quite vanquished him. Then burst his mighty
    heart,
And in his mantle muffling up his face,
Even at the base of Pompey's statue
Which all the while ran blood, great Caesar fell.
O what a fall was there, my countrymen!
Then I, and you, and all of us fell down,

[17] cloak *(in this case, a toga)* [18] *In the Gallic wars
Caesar and his army defeated the tribe of Nervii in 57
B. C.* [19] gash [20] cruelly

83

Whilst bloody treason flourished over us.
O now you weep, and I perceive you feel
The dint [21] of pity. These are gracious drops.
Kind souls, what weep you when you but behold   **200**
Our Caesar's vesture [22] wounded? Look you here!
Here is himself, marred as you see with traitors.

FIRST CITIZEN

O piteous spectacle!

SECOND CITIZEN

O noble Caesar!

THIRD CITIZEN

O woeful day!

FOURTH CITIZEN

O traitors, villains!

FIRST CITIZEN

O most bloody sight!

SECOND CITIZEN

We will be revenged!

CITIZENS

Revenge! About! Seek! Burn! Fire! Kill! Slay!   **210**
Let not a traitor live.

ANTONY

Stay, countrymen.

FIRST CITIZEN

Peace there! Hear the noble Antony.

[21] effect   [22] clothing

84

SECOND CITIZEN

We'll hear him, we'll follow him, we'll die with
him.

ANTONY

Good friends, sweet friends, let me not stir you
up
To such a sudden flood of mutiny.
They that have done this deed are honorable.
What private griefs they have, alas, I know not,
That made them do it. They are wise and
honorable,
And will no doubt with reasons answer you.
I come not, friends, to steal away your hearts.   220
I am no orator as Brutus is;
But, as you know me all, a plain blunt man
That love my friend; and that they know full well
That gave me public leave to speak of him.
For I have neither wit, nor words, nor worth,
Action, nor utterance, nor the power of speech
To stir men's blood. I only speak right on.
I tell you that which you yourselves do know,
Show you sweet Caesar's wounds, poor poor
dumb mouths,
And bid them speak for me. But were I Brutus,   230
And Brutus Antony, there were an Antony
Would ruffle up your spirits, and put a tongue
In every wound of Caesar that should move
The stones of Rome to rise and mutiny.

CITIZENS

We'll mutiny.

FIRST CITIZEN

We'll burn the house of Brutus.

THIRD CITIZEN

Away, then! Come, seek the conspirators.

ANTONY

Yet hear me, countrymen. Yet hear me speak.

CITIZENS

Peace ho! Hear Antony, most noble Antony.

ANTONY

Why, friends, you go to do you know not what.   240
Wherein hath Caesar thus deserved your loves?
Alas, you know not; I must tell you then.
You have forgot the will I told you of.

CITIZENS

Most true, the will! Let's stay and hear the will.

ANTONY

Here is the will, and under Caesar's seal.
To every Roman citizen he gives,
To every several man, seventy-five drachmas![23]

SECOND CITIZEN

Most true, the will! Let's stay and hear the will.

THIRD CITIZEN

O royal Caesar!

ANTONY

Hear me with patience.   250

[23] *To each Roman citizen Caesar left 75 drachmas—about $30.*

CITIZENS

Peace ho!

ANTONY

Moreover, he hath left you all his walks,
His private arbors, and new-planted orchards,
On this side Tiber; he hath left them you,
And to your heirs for ever—common pleasures,
To walk abroad and recreate yourselves.
Here was a Caesar! When comes such another?

FIRST CITIZEN

Never, never. Come, away, away!
We'll burn his body in the holy place,
And with the brands fire the traitors' houses.   260
Take up the body.

SECOND CITIZEN

Go fetch fire!

THIRD CITIZEN

Pluck down benches!

FOURTH CITIZEN

Pluck down forms,²⁴ windows, anything!

Exeunt Citizens with the body.

ANTONY

Now let it work. Mischief, thou art afoot.
Take thou what course thou wilt.

Enter Servant.

How now, fellow?

²⁴ long benches

SERVANT

Sir, Octavius is already come to Rome.

ANTONY

Where is he?

SERVANT

He and Lepidus are at Caesar's house.

ANTONY

And thither will I straight to visit him.   270
He comes upon a wish. Fortune is merry,
And in this mood will give us anything.

SERVANT

I heard him say, Brutus and Cassius
Are rid like madmen through the gates of Rome.

ANTONY

Belike they had some notice of the people,
How I had moved them. Bring me to Octavius.

Exeunt.

ACT THREE, SCENE THREE

*A street near the Forum. Enter
Cinna the poet, and after him Citizens.*

CINNA

I dreamt tonight that I did feast with Caesar,
And things unluckily charge my fantasy.[1]

[1] *And . . . fantasy:* Events give my dreams an unlucky
interpretation

I have no will to wander forth of doors,
Yet something leads me forth.

FIRST CITIZEN

What is your name?

SECOND CITIZEN

Whither are you going?

THIRD CITIZEN

Where do you dwell?

FOURTH CITIZEN

Are you a married man or a bachelor?

SECOND CITIZEN

Answer every man directly.

FIRST CITIZEN

Ay, and briefly.   10

FOURTH CITIZEN

Ay, and wisely.

THIRD CITIZEN

Ay, and truly, you were best.

CINNA

What is my name? Whither am I going? Where
do I dwell? Am I a married man, or a bachelor?
Then to answer every man directly and briefly,
wisely and truly—wisely I say, I am a bachelor.

SECOND CITIZEN

That's as much as to say they are fools that

marry. You'll bear me a bang for that I fear.
Proceed directly.

CINNA

Directly I am going to Caesar's funeral.   20

FIRST CITIZEN

As a friend or an enemy?

CINNA

As a friend.

SECOND CITIZEN

That matter is answered directly.

FOURTH CITIZEN

For your dwelling—briefly.

CINNA

Briefly, I dwell by the Capitol.

THIRD CITIZEN

Your name, sir, truly.

CINNA

Truly, my name is Cinna.

FIRST CITIZEN

Tear him to pieces, he's a conspirator.

CINNA

I am Cinna the poet, I am Cinna the poet.

Fourth Citizen

Tear him for his bad verses, tear him for his   30
bad verses.

Cinna

I am not Cinna the conspirator.

Fourth Citizen

It is no matter, his name's Cinna. Pluck but his
name out of his heart, and turn him going.

Third Citizen

Tear him, tear him! Come, brands ho! Fire-
brands! To Brutus', to Cassius'! Burn all!
Some to Decius' house and some to Casca's; some
to Ligarius'! Away, go!

Exeunt Citizens with the dead body of Cinna.

ACT FOUR, SCENE ONE

Rome, Antony's house. Antony, Octavius, Lepidus.

Antony

These many then shall die. Their names are
pricked.[1]

Octavius

Your brother too must die. Consent you, Lepidus?

Lepidus

I do consent—

[1] marked

OCTAVIUS

        Prick him down, Antony.

LEPIDUS

Upon condition Publius shall not live,
Who is your sister's son, Mark Antony.

ANTONY

He shall not live. Look, with a spot I damn him.
But, Lepidus, go you to Caesar's house.
Fetch the will higher, and we shall determine
How to cut off some charge in legacies.[2]

LEPIDUS

What, shall I find you here?   **10**

OCTAVIUS

Or here or at the Capitol.   *Exit Lepidus.*

ANTONY

This is a slight unmeritable man,
Meet to be sent on errands. Is it fit,
The threefold-world divided,[3] he should stand
One of the three to share it?

OCTAVIUS

        So you thought him,
And took his voice who should be pricked to die
In our black sentence and proscription.

   [2] *Antony plans to change Caesar's will so the Triumvirate will receive more of Caesar's estate.*   [3] *The Triumvirate divided the world into three parts,—Africa, Asia and Europe.*

Antony

Octavius, I have seen more days than you;
And though we lay these honors on this man
To ease ourselves of divers slanderous loads,[4]   20
He shall but bear them as the ass bears gold,
To groan and sweat under the business,
Either led or driven as we point the way;
And having brought our treasure where we will,
Then take we down his load, and turn him off,
Like to the empty ass, to shake his ears
And graze in commons.[5]

Octavius

              You may do your will.
But he's a tried and valiant soldier.

Antony

So is my horse, Octavius, and for that
I do appoint him store of provender.   30
It is a creature that I teach to fight,
To wind,[6] to stop, to run directly on,
His corporal [7] motion governed by my spirit.
And in some taste,[8] is Lepidus but so;
He must be taught, and trained, and bid go
   forth.
A barren-spirited fellow; one that feeds
On objects, arts, and imitations
Which, out of use and staled by other men,
Begin his fashion.[9] Do not talk of him
But as a property. And now, Octavius,   40

---

[4] *To . . . loads:* to share the blame   [5] public pasture
[6] turn   [7] bodily   [8] degree   [9] *one . . . fashion:* one
that lives in an artificial way by imitating worn-out fashions

Listen great things. Brutus and Cassius
Are levying powers; we must straight make
    head.[10]
Therefore let our alliance be combined,
Our best friends made, our means stretched; [11]
And let us presently go sit in council
How covert matters may be best disclosed
And open perils surest answered.

OCTAVIUS

Let us do so, for we are at the stake [12]
And bayed about with many enemies;
And some that smile have in their hearts, I fear,   50
Millions of mischiefs.   *Exeunt.*

ACT FOUR, SCENE TWO

> *The camp near Sardis. Before Brutus'
> tent. Drum. Enter Brutus, Lucius,
> Lucilius, and Soldiers. Titinius and
> Pindarus meet them.*

BRUTUS

Stand ho!

LUCILIUS

Give the word ho, and stand!

BRUTUS

What now, Lucilius, is Cassius near?

---

[10] *make head:* raise an army   [11] fully used   [12] *In the
Elizabethan sport of bear-baiting, a bear tied to a stake
was attacked by dogs.*

94

LUCILIUS

He is at hand, and Pindarus is come
To do you salutation from his master.

BRUTUS

He greets me well. Your master, Pindarus,
In his own change,[1] or by ill officers,
Hath given me some worthy cause to wish
Things done, undone. But if he be at hand
I shall be satisfied.

PINDARUS

        I do not doubt   10
But that my noble master will appear
Such as he is, full of regard and honor.

BRUTUS

He is not doubted. A word, Lucilius,
How he received you. Let me be resolved.[2]

LUCILIUS

With courtesy and with respect enough,
But not with such familiar instances,[3]
Nor with such free and friendly conference
As he hath used of old.

BRUTUS

        Thou hast described
A hot friend cooling. Ever note, Lucilius,
When love begins to sicken and decay   20
It useth an enforced ceremony.
There are no tricks in plain and simple faith;

[1] *In . . . change*: through a change in his feelings
[2]informed [3] *familiar instances:* friendly gestures

But hollow men, like horses hot at hand,
Make gallant show and promise of their mettle;
But when they should endure the bloody spur,
They fall their crests, and like deceitful jades
Sink in the trial.[4] Comes his army on?

LUCILIUS

They mean this night in Sardis to be quartered.
The greater part, the horse in general,
Are come with Cassius.   *Low march within.*

BRUTUS

       Hark, he is arrived.   30
March gently on to meet him.

Enter Cassius and his Soldiers.

CASSIUS

Stand ho!

BRUTUS

Stand ho! Speak the word along.

FIRST SOLDIER

Stand!

SECOND SOLDIER

Stand!

THIRD SOLDIER

Stand!

[4] *They fall . . . trial:* They let their necks droop and,
like weary nags, fail the test

CASSIUS

Most noble brother, you have done me wrong.

BRUTUS

Judge me, you gods. Wrong I mine enemies?
And if not so, how should I wrong a brother?

CASSIUS

Brutus, this sober form of yours hides wrongs,   40
And when you do them—

BRUTUS

            Cassius, be content.[5]
Speak your griefs softly. I do know you well.
Before the eyes of both our armies here,
Which should perceive nothing but love from us,
Let us not wrangle. Bid them move away.
Then in my tent, Cassius, enlarge your griefs,
And I will give you audience.

CASSIUS

            Pindarus,
Bid our commanders lead their charges off
A little from this ground.

BRUTUS

Lucius, do you the like, and let no man   50
Come to our tent till we have done our
   conference.

Let Lucilius and Titinius guard our door.

     Exeunt Lucius, Pindarus and Soldiers.
     Brutus and Cassius enter the tent.

[5] calm

97

ACT FOUR, SCENE THREE

Within the tent.

CASSIUS

That you have wronged me doth appear in this:
You have condemned and noted [1] Lucius Pella
For taking bribes here of the Sardians;
Wherein my letters, praying on his side,
Because I knew the man, were slighted off.[2]

BRUTUS

You wronged yourself to write in such a case.

CASSIUS

In such a time as this it is not meet
That every nice [3] offense should bear his
    comment.

BRUTUS

Let me tell you, Cassius, you yourself
Are much condemned to have an itching palm,   10
To sell and mart your offices for gold
To undeservers.

CASSIUS

   I, an itching palm?
You know that you are Brutus that speaks this,
Or, by the gods, this speech were else your last!

BRUTUS

The name of Cassius honors this corruption,

---

[1] slandered   [2] dismissed   [3] small

And chastisement doth therefore hide his head.

Chastisement?

Remember March, the ides of March remember.
Did not great Julius bleed for justice' sake?
What villain touched his body that did stab   20
And not for justice? What, shall one of us,
That struck the foremost man of all this world
But for supporting robbers,—shall we now
Contaminate our fingers with base bribes,
And sell the mighty space of our large honors
For so much trash as may be grasped thus?
I had rather be a dog and bay the moon
Than such a Roman.

Brutus, bait not me!
I'll not endure it. You forget yourself
To hedge me in! ⁴ I am a soldier, I,   30
Older in practice, abler than yourself
To make conditions.

Go to! You are not, Cassius.

I am.

I say you are not.

⁴ *To hedge me in*: to try to cut down my authority

99

CASSIUS

Urge me no more! I shall forget myself.
Have mind upon your health. Tempt me no
  farther.

BRUTUS

Away, slight man!

CASSIUS

Is't possible?

BRUTUS

Hear me, for I will speak.
Must I give way and room to your rash choler? [5]
Shall I be frighted when a madman stares?   40

CASSIUS

O ye gods, ye gods! Must I endure all this?

BRUTUS

All this? Ay, more. Fret till your proud heart
  break.
Go show your slaves how choleric you are,
And make your bondmen tremble. Must I budge?
Must I observe [6] you? Must I stand and crouch
Under your testy humor? By the gods,
You shall digest the venom of your spleen,
Though it do split you. For from this day forth,
I'll use you for my mirth, yea for my laughter,
When you are waspish.

CASSIUS

Is it come to this?   50

[5] anger [6] respect

BRUTUS

You say you are a better soldier.
Let it appear so. Make your vaunting [7] true,
And it shall please me well. For mine own part,
I shall be glad to learn of noble men.

CASSIUS

You wrong me every way! You wrong me, Brutus!
I said, an elder soldier, not a better.
Did I say "better"?

BRUTUS

If you did, I care not.

CASSIUS

When Caesar lived, he durst not thus have moved
me,

BRUTUS

Peace, peace, you durst not so have tempted him.

CASSIUS

I durst not?   60

BRUTUS

No.

CASSIUS

What, durst not tempt him?

BRUTUS

For your life you durst not.

[7] boasting

Do not presume too much upon my love.
I may do that I shall be sorry for.

You have done that you should be sorry for.
There is no terror, Cassius, in your threats;
For I am armed so strong in honesty
That they pass by me, as the idle wind,
Which I respect not. I did send to you
For certain sums of gold, which you denied me;   70
For I can raise no money by vile means.
By heaven, I had rather coin my heart
And drop my blood for drachmas than to wring
From the hard hands of peasants their vile trash
By any indirection.[8] I did send
To you for gold to pay my legions,
Which you denied me. Was that done like
    Cassius?
Should I have answered Caius Cassius so?
When Marcus Brutus grows so covetous
To lock such rascal counters [9] from his friends,   80
Be ready gods with all your thunderbolts;
Dash him to pieces!

I denied you not.

You did.

I did not. He was but a fool that brought

[8] trickery   [9] cheap coins

My answer back. Brutus hath rived [10] my heart.
A friend should bear his friend's infirmities,
But Brutus makes mine greater than they are.

BRUTUS

I do not, till you practice them on me.

CASSIUS

You love me not.

BRUTUS

I do not like your faults.

CASSIUS

A friendly eye could never see such faults.   90

BRUTUS

A flatterer's would not, though they do appear
As huge as high Olympus

CASSIUS

Come, Antony, and young Octavius, come!
Revenge yourselves alone on Cassius,
For Cassius is aweary of the world—
Hated by one he loves, braved [11] by his brother,
Checked like a bondman,[12] all his faults observed,
Set in a note book, learned, and conned by rote [13]
To cast into my teeth. O I could weep
My spirit from mine eyes. There is my dagger,   100
And here my naked breast; within, a heart
Dearer than Pluto's mine,[14] richer than gold.

---

[10] split   [11] defied   [12] slave   [13] *conned by rote:* mem-
orized   [14] *Pluto, god of the underworld, controlled all
riches in the earth.*

If that thou beest a Roman, take it forth.
I that denied thee gold, will give my heart.
Strike as thou didst at Caesar. For I know,
When thou didst hate him worst, thou lovedst
 him better
Than ever thou lovedst Cassius.

BRUTUS

            Sheathe your dagger.
Be angry when you will, it shall have scope.
Do what you will, dishonor shall be humor.[15]
O Cassius, you are yoked with a lamb   110
That carries anger as the flint bears fire,
Who much enforced [16] shows a hasty spark,
And straight is cold again.

CASSIUS

           Hath Cassius lived
To be but mirth and laughter to his Brutus
When grief and blood ill-tempered vexeth him?

BRUTUS

When I spoke that, I was ill-tempered too.

CASSIUS

Do you confess so much? Give me your hand.

BRUTUS

And my heart too.

CASSIUS

O Brutus!

15 *dishonor . . . humor*: your insults will be interpreted
as only bad temper   16 provoked

BRUTUS

What's the matter?

CASSIUS

Have you not love enough to bear with me
When that rash humor which my mother gave me   120
Makes me forgetful?

BRUTUS

Yes, Cassius, and from henceforth,
When you are over-earnest with your Brutus,
He'll think your mother chides, and leave you so.

Enter Poet, and Lucius following.

POET

Let me go in to see the generals.
There is some grudge between 'em. 'Tis not meet
They be alone.

LUCIUS

You shall not come to them.

POET

Nothing but death shall stay me.

CASSIUS

How now? What's the matter?

POET

For shame, you generals, what do you mean?
Love, and be friends, as two such men should be;   130
For I have seen more years, I'm sure, than ye.

105

CASSIUS

Ha, ha, how vilely doth this cynic rhyme!

BRUTUS

Get you hence, sirrah. Saucy fellow, hence!

CASSIUS

Bear with him, Brutus; 'tis his fashion.

BRUTUS

I'll know his humor when he knows his time.
What should the wars do with these jigging [17]
    fools?
Companion, hence!

CASSIUS

Away, away, be gone.

Exit Poet.

BRUTUS

Lucilius and Titinius, bid the commanders
Prepare to lodge their companies tonight.

CASSIUS

And come yourselves, and bring Messala with   140
    you
Immediately to us.

Exeunt Lucilius and Titinius.

BRUTUS

Lucius, a bowl of wine.

Exit Lucius.

[17] rhyming

CASSIUS

I did not think you could have been so angry.

BRUTUS

O Cassius, I am sick of many griefs.

CASSIUS

Of your philosophy you make no use
If you give place to accidental evils.[18]

BRUTUS

No man bears sorrow better. Portia is dead.

CASSIUS

Ha! Portia?

BRUTUS

She is dead.

CASSIUS

How 'scaped I killing when I crossed you so?
O insupportable and touching loss!   150
Upon what sickness?

BRUTUS

              Impatient of my absence,
And grief that young Octavius with Mark
   Antony
Have made themselves so strong—for with her
   death

---

[18] *As a Stoic, Brutus should not be disturbed by mere
bad luck or misfortune.*

That tidings came. With this she fell distract
And, her attendants absent, swallowed fire.

CASSIUS

And died so?

BRUTUS

Even so.

CASSIUS

O ye immortal gods!

Enter Lucius, with wine and tapers.

BRUTUS

Speak no more of her. Give me a bowl of wine.
In this I bury all unkindness, Cassius.

CASSIUS

My heart is thirsty for that noble pledge.
Fill, Lucius, till the wine o'erswell the cup.   160
I cannot drink too much of Brutus' love.

Exit Lucius.

Enter Titinius and Messala.

BRUTUS

Come in, Titinius. Welcome, good Messala.
Now sit we close about this taper here
And call in question [19] our necessities.

CASSIUS

Portia, art thou gone?

[19] *call in question:* discuss

BRUTUS

No more, I pray you.
Messala, I have here received letters
That young Octavius and Mark Antony
Come down upon us with a mighty power,
Bending their expedition toward Philippi.[20]

MESSALA

Myself have letters of the selfsame tenor.   170

BRUTUS

With what addition?

MESSALA

That by proscription and bills of outlawry,
Octavius, Antony, and Lepidus
Have put to death an hundred senators.

BRUTUS

Therein our letters do not well agree.
Mine speak of seventy senators that died
By their proscriptions, Cicero being one.

CASSIUS

Cicero one?

MESSALA

Cicero is dead,
And by that order of proscription.
Had you your letters from your wife, my lord?   180

BRUTUS

No, Messala.

[20] *Philippi was an ancient city in northern Greece.*

MESSALA

Nor nothing in your letters writ of her?

BRUTUS

Nothing, Messala.

MESSALA

That, methinks, is strange.

BRUTUS

Why ask you? Hear you aught of her in yours?

MESSALA

No, my lord.

BRUTUS

Now as you are a Roman, tell me true.

MESSALA

Then like a Roman bear the truth I tell:
For certain she is dead, and by strange manner.

BRUTUS

Why, farewell, Portia. We must die, Messala. 190
With meditating that she must die once,
I have the patience to endure it now.

MESSALA

Even so great men great losses should endure.

CASSIUS

I have as much of this in art as you,
But yet my nature could not bear it so.[21]

21 *I have . . . so*: I know the theory of Stoicism as well
as you, but my heart would not let me practice it

110

BRUTUS

Well, to our work alive. What do you think
Of marching to Philippi presently?

CASSIUS

I do not think it good.

BRUTUS

       Your reason?

CASSIUS

              This it is:
'Tis better that the enemy seek us.
So shall he waste his means, weary his soldiers,
Doing himself offense, whilst we, lying still,   200
Are full of rest, defense, and nimbleness.

BRUTUS

Good reasons must of force give place to better.
The people 'twixt Philippi and this ground
Do stand but [22] in a forced affection,
For they have grudged us contribution.
The enemy, marching along by them,
By them shall make a fuller number up,
Come on refreshed, new-added, and encouraged;
From which advantage shall we cut him off
If at Philippi we do face him there,   210
These people at our back.

CASSIUS

           Hear me, good brother.

BRUTUS

Under your pardon. You must note beside

[22] *Do stand but*: regard us with

111

That we have tried the utmost of our friends;
Our legions are brimful, our cause is ripe.
The enemy increaseth every day;
We, at the height, are ready to decline.
There is a tide in the affairs of men,
Which taken at the flood leads on to fortune;
Omitted, all the voyage of their life
Is bound in shallows and in miseries.   220
On such a full sea are we now afloat,
And we must take the current when it serves,
Or lose our ventures.

CASSIUS

              Then with your will go on.
We'll along ourselves, and meet them at Philippi.

BRUTUS

The deep of night is crept upon our talk
And nature must obey necessity,
Which we will niggard [23] with a little rest.
There is no more to say?

CASSIUS

              No more. Good night:
Early tomorrow will we rise and hence.[24]

BRUTUS

Lucius! *[Enter Lucius.]* My gown. *Exit Lucius.*   230
Farewell, good Messala.
Good night, Titinius. Noble, noble Cassius,
Good night and good repose.

CASSIUS

              O my dear brother,

[23] cut short   [24] go

This was an ill beginning of the night.
Never come such division 'tween our souls!
Let it not, Brutus.

Enter Lucius, with the gown.

BRUTUS

Everything is well.

CASSIUS

Good night, my lord.

BRUTUS

Good night, good brother.

TITINIUS *and* MESSALA

Good night, Lord Brutus.

BRUTUS

Farewell every one.

Exeunt Cassius, Titinius, and Messala.

Give me the gown. Where is thy instrument? [25]

LUCIUS

Here in the tent.

BRUTUS

What, thou speakest drowsily? **240**
Poor knave, I blame thee not; thou art o'er-
watched.
Call Claudius and some other of my men;
I'll have them sleep on cushions in my tent.

[25] *i.e.,* a lute

LUCIUS

Varro and Claudius!

Enter Varro and Claudius.

VARRO

Calls my lord?

BRUTUS

I pray you, sirs, lie in my tent and sleep;
It may be I shall raise [26] you by and by
On business to my brother Cassius.

VARRO

So please you, we will stand and watch your
  pleasure.

BRUTUS

I will not have it so. Lie down, good sirs;   250
It may be I shall otherwise bethink me.
Look, Lucius, here's the book I sought for so;
I put it in the pocket of my gown.

LUCIUS

I was sure your lordship did not give it me.

BRUTUS

Bear with me, good boy, I am much forgetful.
Canst thou hold up thy heavy eyes a while,
And touch thy instrument a strain or two?

LUCIUS

Ay, my lord, an't please you.

[26] wake

BRUTUS

It does, my boy.
I trouble thee too much, but thou art willing.

LUCIUS

It is my duty, sir. 260

BRUTUS

I should not urge thy duty past thy might;
I know young bloods look for a time of rest.

LUCIUS

I have slept, my lord, already.

BRUTUS

It was well done, and thou shalt sleep again;
I will not hold thee long. If I do live,
I will be good to thee.   *Music, and a song.*
This is a sleepy tune. O murderous slumber,
Layest thou thy leaden mace upon my boy,
That plays thee music? Gentle knave, good night.
I will not do thee so much wrong to wake thee. 270
If thou dost nod, thou breakest thy instrument;
I'll take it from thee, and, good boy, good night.
Let me see, let me see. Is not the leaf turned
  down
Where I left reading? Here it is, I think.   *Sits.*

Enter the Ghost of Caesar.

How ill this taper burns! Ha! Who comes here?
I think it is the weakness of mine eyes
That shapes this monstrous apparition.
It comes upon me. Art thou any thing?

Art thou some god, some angel, or some devil,
That makest my blood cold and my hair to
    stare? [27]   280
Speak to me what thou art.

GHOST OF CAESAR

Thy evil spirit, Brutus.

BRUTUS

              Why comest thou?

GHOST OF CAESAR

To tell thee thou shalt see me at Philippi.

BRUTUS

Well; then I shall see thee again?

GHOST OF CAESAR

Ay, at Philippi.

BRUTUS

Why, I will see thee at Philippi then. *Exit Ghost.*
Now I have taken heart thou vanishest.
Ill spirit, I would hold more talk with thee.
Boy, Lucius! Varro! Claudius! Sirs, awake!
Claudius!   290

LUCIUS

The strings, my lord, are false.

BRUTUS

He thinks he still is at his instrument.
Lucius, awake.

[27] stand on end

116

LUCIUS

My lord?

BRUTUS

Didst thou dream Lucius, that thou so criedst
out?

LUCIUS

My lord, I do not know that I did cry.

BRUTUS

Yes, that thou didst. Didst thou see anything?

LUCIUS

Nothing, my lord.

BRUTUS

Sleep again, Lucius. Sirrah Claudius!
[To Varro.] Fellow thou, awake!   300

VARRO

My lord?

CLAUDIUS

My lord?

BRUTUS

Why did you so cry out, sirs, in your sleep?

VARRO *and* CLAUDIUS

Did we, my lord?

BRUTUS

Ay. Saw you anything?

No, my lord, I saw nothing.

Nor I, my lord.

Go and commend me to my brother Cassius.
Bid him set on his powers betimes before,
And we will follow.

It shall be done, my lord.

Exeunt.

ACT FIVE, SCENE ONE

A plain near Philippi. Enter Octavius, Antony, and their Soldiers.

Now, Antony, our hopes are answered.
You said the enemy would not come down,
But keep the hills and upper regions.
It proves not so. Their battles [1] are at hand;
They mean to warn [2] us at Philippi here,
Answering before we do demand of them.

Tut, I am in their bosoms and I know
Wherefore they do it. They could be content
To visit other places, and come down

[1] armies   [2] challenge

With fearful bravery, thinking by this face   10
To fasten in our thoughts that they have
    courage;[3]
But 'tis not so.

       Enter Messenger.

MESSENGER

     Prepare you, generals.
The enemy comes on in gallant show.
Their bloody sign of battle is hung out,
And something to be done immediately.

ANTONY

Octavius, lead your battle softly on
Upon the left hand of the even field.

OCTAVIUS

Upon the right hand I. Keep thou the left.

ANTONY

Why do you cross me in this exigent? [4]

OCTAVIUS

I do not cross you; but I will do so. *March. Drum.*   20

    Enter Brutus, Cassius, and their Soldiers;
    Lucilius, Titinius, Messala, and others.

BRUTUS

They stand and would have parley.

CASSIUS

Stand fast, Titinius. We must out and talk.

   [3] *They could . . . courage*: although they would rather
not fight at all, they will try to convince us of their
courage by charging at us   [4] crisis

OCTAVIUS

Mark Antony, shall we give sign of battle?

ANTONY

No, Caesar, we will answer on their charge.[5]
Make forth. The generals would have some
words.

OCTAVIUS

Stir not until the signal.

BRUTUS

Words before blows: is it so, countrymen?

OCTAVIUS

Not that we love words better, as you do.

BRUTUS

Good words are better than bad strokes,
Octavius.

ANTONY

In your bad strokes, Brutus, you give good
words: 30
Witness the hole you made in Caesar's heart,
Crying "Long live! Hail Caesar!"

CASSIUS

Antony,
The posture [6] of your blows are yet unknown;
But for your words, they rob the Hybla [7] bees,
And leave them honeyless.

[5] *answer . . . charge*: fight when they attack   [6] style
[7] *Hybla was a town in Sicily famous for especially
sweet honey.*

120

ANTONY

Not stingless too.

BRUTUS

O yes, and soundless too.
For you have stolen their buzzing, Antony,
And very wisely threat before you sting.

ANTONY

Villains! You did not so when your vile daggers
Hacked one another in the sides of Caesar.   40
You showed your teeth like apes, and fawned like
    hounds,
And bowed like bondmen, kissing Caesar's feet;
Whilst damned Casca, like a cur, behind
Struck Caesar on the neck. O you flatterers!

CASSIUS

Flatterers? Now, Brutus, thank yourself;
This tongue had not offended so today,
If Cassius might have ruled.

OCTAVIUS

Come, come, the cause. If arguing make us sweat,
The proof of it will turn to redder drops.
Look,   50
I draw a sword against conspirators:
When think you that the sword goes up [8] again?
Never, till Caesar's three and thirty wounds
Be well avenged or till another Caesar
Have added slaughter to the sword of traitors.

[8] *goes up*: will be sheathed

BRUTUS

Caesar, thou canst not die by traitors' hands,
Unless thou bringest them with thee.

OCTAVIUS

So I hope.
I was not born to die on Brutus' sword.

BRUTUS

O if thou wert the noblest of thy strain,
Young man, thou couldst not die more honorable.   **60**

CASSIUS

A peevish schoolboy, worthless of such honor,
Joined with a masker and a reveller.

ANTONY

Old Cassius still.

OCTAVIUS

Come, Antony, away!
Defiance, traitors, hurl we in your teeth.
If you dare fight today, come to the field;
If not, when you have stomachs.

Exeunt Octavius, Antony, and Soldiers.

CASSIUS

Why, now blow wind, swell billow, and swim
    bark!
The storm is up, and all is on the hazard.[9]

[9] *on the hazard:* at stake

BRUTUS

Ho, Lucilius! Hark, a word with you.

LUCILIUS

My lord?
They speak apart.

CASSIUS

Messala.

MESSALA

What says my general?

CASSIUS

Messala,   70
This is my birthday; as this very day
Was Cassius born. Give me thy hand, Messala.
Be thou my witness that against my will,
As Pompey was, am I compelled to set
Upon one battle all our liberties.
You know that I held Epicurus strong,
And his opinion.[10] Now I change my mind,
And partly credit things that do presage.[11]
Coming from Sardis, on our former ensign [12]
Two mighty eagles fell; and there they perched,   80
Gorging and feeding from our soldiers' hands,
Who to Philippi here consorted [13] us.
This morning are they fled away and gone,
And in their steads do ravens, crows, and kites
Fly o'er our heads and downward look on us
As we were sickly prey. Their shadows seem

---

[10] *Cassius was formerly an Epicurean, a materialist who did not believe in omens* [11] foretell [12] standard
[13] accompanied

A canopy most fatal, under which
Our army lies, ready to give up the ghost.

MESSALA

Believe not so.

CASSIUS

I but believe it partly,
For I am fresh of spirit and resolved
To meet all perils very constantly.

90

BRUTUS

Even so, Lucilius.

CASSIUS

Now, most noble Brutus,
The gods today stand friendly, that we may,
Lovers in peace, lead on our days to age.
But since the affairs of men rest still incertain,
Let's reason with the worst that may befall.
If we do lose this battle, then is this
The very last time we shall speak together.
What are you then determined to do?

BRUTUS

Even by the rule of that philosophy [14]
By which I did blame Cato for the death
Which he did give himself—I know not how,
But I do find it cowardly and vile,
For fear of what might fall, so to prevent [15]
The time [16] of life—arming myself with patience
To stay [17] the providence of some high powers

100

---

[14] *i.e.*, Stoicism   [15] hasten   [16] end   [17] wait for

That govern us below.[18]

CASSIUS

          Then, if we lose this battle,
You are contented to be led in triumph
Through the streets of Rome?

BRUTUS

No, Cassius, no. Think not, thou noble Roman,   **110**
That ever Brutus will go bound to Rome.
He bears too great a mind. But this same day
Must end that work the ides of March begun,
And whether we shall meet again I know not.
Therefore our everlasting farewell take.
For ever, and for ever, farewell, Cassius.
If we do meet again, why, we shall smile;
If not, why then this parting was well made.

CASSIUS

For ever, and for ever, farewell, Brutus.
If we do meet again, we'll smile indeed;   **120**
If not, 'tis true this parting was well made.

BRUTUS

Why then, lead on. O that a man might know
The end of this day's business ere it come.
But it sufficeth that the day will end,
And then the end is known. Come ho, away!

Exeunt.

[18] *I know . . . below*: I find suicide a coward's way out;
(if I should lose the battle) I will try to meet my fate
patiently

ACT FIVE, SCENE TWO

The same. Alarums.
Enter Brutus and Messala.

BRUTUS

Ride, ride, Messala, ride and give these bills [1]
Unto the legions on the other side.   *Alarum.*
Let them set on at once; for I perceive
But cold demeanor in Octavius' wing,
And sudden push gives them the overthrow.
Ride, ride, Messala. Let them all come down.

                              Exeunt.

ACT FIVE, SCENE THREE

The same. Alarums.
Enter Cassius and Titinius.

CASSIUS

O look, Titinius, look, the villains fly.
Myself have to mine own turned enemy:
This ensign here of mine was turning back;
I slew the coward, and did take it [1] from him.

TITINIUS

O Cassius, Brutus gave the word too early,
Who having some advantage on Octavius,
Took it too eagerly. His soldiers fell to spoil [2]
Whilst we by Antony are all enclosed.

[1] orders   [1] *i.e.*, the ensign, or standard   [2] looting

126

Enter Pindarus.

PINDARUS

Fly further off, my lord, fly further off!
Mark Antony is in your tents, my lord.   **10**
Fly, therefore, noble Cassius, fly far off.

CASSIUS

This hill is far enough. Look, look, Titinius;
Are those my tents where I perceive the fire?

TITINIUS

They are, my lord.

CASSIUS

        Titinius, if thou lovest me,
Mount thou my horse and hide thy spurs in him
Till he have brought thee up to yonder troops
And here again, that I may rest assured
Whether yond troops are friend or enemy.

TITINIUS

I will be here again even with a thought.   *Exit.*

CASSIUS

Go, Pindarus, get higher on that hill.   **20**
My sight was ever thick.[3] Regard Titinius,
And tell me what thou notest about the field.

               Pindarus goes up.

This day I breathed first. Time is come round,
And where I did begin, there shall I end.
My life is run his compass. Sirrah, what news?

[3] poor

127

PINDARUS [*above*]

O my lord!

CASSIUS

What news?

PINDARUS

Titinius is enclosed round about
With horsemen that make to him on the spur,
Yet he spurs on. Now they are almost on him.　　30
Now, Titinius! Now some light.[4] O he lights too.
He's ta'en.[5] [*Shout*] And hark! they shout for joy.

CASSIUS

Come down; behold no more.
O coward that I am to live so long,
To see my best friend ta'en before my face.

Pindarus descends.

Come hither, sirrah.
In Parthia did I take thee prisoner;
And then I swore thee, saving of thy life,
That whatsoever I did bid thee do,
Thou shouldst attempt it. Come now, keep thine
　　oath.　　40
Now be a freeman, and with this good sword,
That ran through Caesar's bowels, search this
　　bosom.
Stand not to answer. Here, take thou the hilts,
And when my face is covered, as 'tis now,
Guide thou the sword.—Caesar, thou art revenged
Even with the sword that killed thee.　　*Dies.*

---

[4] dismount　　[5] taken, captured

128

PINDARUS

So, I am free; yet would not so have been,
Durst I have done my will. O Cassius!
Far from this country Pindarus shall run,
Where never Roman shall take note of him. *Exit.*   50

Enter Titinius and Messala.

MESSALA

It is but change,[6] Titinius; for Octavius
Is overthrown by noble Brutus' power,
As Cassius' legions are by Antony.

TITINIUS

These tidings will well comfort Cassius.

MESSALA

Where did you leave him?

TITINIUS

                        All disconsolate,
With Pindarus his bondman, on this hill.

MESSALA

Is not that he that lies upon the ground?

TITINIUS

He lies not like the living. O my heart!

MESSALA

Is not that he?

  [6] exchange

129

TITINIUS

No, this was he, Messala.
But Cassius is no more. O setting sun,60
As in thy red rays thou dost sink to night,
So in his red blood Cassius' day is set!
The sun of Rome is set. Our day is gone;
Clouds, dews, and dangers come; our deeds are
    done.
Mistrust of my success hath done this deed.

MESSALA

Mistrust of good success hath done this deed.
O hateful error, melancholy's child,
Why dost thou show to the apt thoughts of men
The things that are not? O error soon conceived,70
Thou never comest unto a happy birth,
But killest the mother that engendered thee.

TITINIUS

What, Pindarus! Where art thou, Pindarus?

MESSALA

Seek him, Titinius, whilst I go to meet
The noble Brutus, thrusting this report
Into his ears. I may say "thrusting" it,
For piercing steel and darts envenomed
Shall be as welcome to the ears of Brutus
As tidings of this sight.

TITINIUS

        Hie you, Messala,
And I will seek for Pindarus the while.

Exit Messala.

Why didst thou send me forth, brave Cassius? **80**
Did I not meet thy friends, and did not they
Put on my brows this wreath of victory
And bid me give it thee? Didst thou not hear
 their shouts?
Alas, thou has misconstrued everything!
But hold thee, take this garland on thy brow.
Thy Brutus bid me give it thee, and I
Will do his bidding. Brutus, come apace
And see how I regarded Caius Cassius.
By your leave, gods—this is a Roman's part.
Come Cassius' sword and find Titinius' heart. **90**

Dies.

*Alarum. Enter Brutus, Messala, Young
Cato,[7] Strato, Volumnius, Lucilius, and
others.*

BRUTUS

Where, where, Messala, doth his body lie?

MESSALA

Lo, yonder, and Titinius mourning it.

BRUTUS

Titinius' face is upward.

CATO

He is slain.

BRUTUS

O Julius Caesar, thou are mighty yet;
Thy spirit walks abroad and turns our swords
In our own proper entrails.   *Low alarums.*

[7] *Young Cato was Portia's brother, thus Brutus' broth-
er-in-law.*

131

CATO

Brave Titinius!
Look whether he have not crowned dead Cassius.

BRUTUS

Are yet two Romans living such as these?
The last of all the Romans, fare thee well.
It is impossible that ever Rome   **100**
Should breed thy fellow. Friends, I owe more
   tears
To this dead man than you shall see me pay.
I shall find time, Cassius; I shall find time.
Come therefore, and to Thasos [8] send his body.
His funerals shall not be in our camp,
Lest it discomfort us. Lucilius, come,
And come, young Cato. Let us to the field.
Labeo and Flavius set our battles on.
'Tis three o'clock; and, Romans, yet ere night
We shall try fortune in a second fight. *Exeunt.* **110**

ACT FIVE, SCENE FOUR

The same. Alarum. Enter Brutus, Messala,
Young Cato, Lucilius, Flavius, and
Soldiers, fighting.

BRUTUS

Yet, countrymen, O yet hold up your heads.

Exit, fighting, followed by Messala.

CATO

What bastard doth not? Who will go with me?

[8] *Thasos is an island in the Aegean Sea.*

132

I will proclaim my name about the field—
I am the son of Marcus Cato, ho!
A foe to tyrants, and my country's friend.
I am the son of Marcus Cato, ho!

Enter more Soldiers fighting.

LUCILIUS

And I am Brutus, Marcus Brutus I;
Brutus, my country's friend. Know me for Brutus!

Cato is slain.

O young and noble Cato, art thou down?
Why now thou diest as bravely as Titinius,   10
And mayst be honored, being Cato's son.

FIRST SOLDIER

Yield, or thou diest.

LUCILIUS

Only I yield to die.
There is so much, that thou wilt kill me straight:

Offers money.

Kill Brutus, and be honored in his death.

FIRST SOLDIER

We must not. A noble prisoner!

SECOND SOLDIER

Room ho! Tell Antony, Brutus is ta'en.

Enter Antony.

FIRST SOLDIER

I'll tell the news. Here comes the general.

133

Brutus is ta'en, Brutus is ta'en my lord.

Where is he?

LUCILIUS

Safe, Antony; Brutus is safe enough.   **20**
I dare assure thee that no enemy
Shall ever take alive the noble Brutus.
The gods defend him from so great a shame.
When you do find him, or alive or dead,
He will be found like Brutus, like himself.

ANTONY

This is not Brutus, friend, but I assure you,
A prize no less in worth. Keep this man safe;
Give him all kindness. I had rather have
Such men my friends than enemies. Go on
And see whether Brutus be alive or dead,   **30**
And bring us word unto Octavius' tent
How everything is chanced.   *Exeunt.*

ACT FIVE, SCENE FIVE

*The same. Enter Brutus, Dardanius,
Clitus, Strato, and Volumnius.*

BRUTUS

Come, poor remains of friends, rest on this rock.

CLITUS

Statilius [1] showed the torchlight, but, my lord,

---

[1] *Statilius was a scout who reached Antony's camp and signaled, but did not return.*

He came not back: he is or ta'en or slain.

BRUTUS

Sit thee down, Clitus. Slaying is the word.
It is a deed in fashion. Hark thee, Clitus.

Whispers.

CLITUS

What, I, my lord? No, not for all the world.

BRUTUS

Peace then, no words.

CLITUS

I'll rather kill myself.

BRUTUS

Hark thee, Dardanius.   *Whispers.*

DARDANIUS

Shall I do such a deed?

CLITUS

O Dardanius!

DARDANIUS

O Clitus!   10

CLITUS

What ill request did Brutus make to thee?

DARDANIUS

To kill him, Clitus. Look, he meditates.

135

CLITUS

Now is that noble vessel full of grief,
That it runs over even at his eyes.

BRUTUS

Come hither, good Volumnius. List a word.

VOLUMNIUS

What says, my lord?

BRUTUS

            Why this, Volumnius.
The ghost of Caesar hath appeared to me
Two several [2] times by night—at Sardis once,
And this last night here in Philippi fields.
I know my hour is come.

VOLUMNIUS

           Not so, my lord.   **20**

BRUTUS

Nay I am sure it is, Volumnius.
Thou seest the world, Volumnius, how it goes.
Our enemies have beat us to the pit.

                    Low alarums.

It is more worthy to leap in ourselves
Than tarry till they push us. Good Volumnius,
Thou knowest that we two went to school
   together;
Even for that our love of old, I prithee
Hold thou my sword-hilts, whilst I run on it.

[2] different

136

VOLUMNIUS

That's not an office for a friend, my lord.

Alarum still.

CLITUS

Fly, fly, my lord, there is no tarrying here.　　　30

BRUTUS

Farewell to you; and you; and you, Volumnius.
Strato, thou hast been all this while asleep;
Farewell to thee too, Strato. Countrymen,
My heart doth joy that yet in all my life
I found no man but he was true to me.
I shall have glory by this losing day,
More than Octavius and Mark Antony
By this vile conquest shall attain unto.
So fare you well at once, for Brutus' tongue
Hath almost ended his life's history.　　　40
Night hangs upon mine eyes; my bones would
　rest
That have but labored to attain this hour.

Alarums. Cry within, Fly, fly, fly!

CLITUS

Fly, my lord, fly!

BRUTUS

Hence! I will follow.

*Exeunt Clitus, Dardanius,
and Volumnius.*

I prithee, Strato, stay thou by thy lord.

137

Thou art a fellow of a good respect;
Thy life hath had some smatch [3] of honor in it.
Hold then my sword and turn away thy face
While I do run upon it. Wilt thou, Strato?

STRATO

Give me your hand first. Fare you well, my lord.

BRUTUS

Farewell, good Strato.   *Runs on his sword.*
                  Caesar, now be still.   50
I killed not thee with half so good a will.

                                    Dies.

> *Alarum. Retreat. Enter Octavius, Antony, Messala, Lucilius, and Soldiers.*

OCTAVIUS

What man is that?

MESSALA

My master's man. Strato, where is thy master?

STRATO

Free from the bondage you are in, Messala;
The conquerors can but make a fire of him,
For Brutus only overcame himself,
And no man else hath honor by his death.

LUCILIUS

So Brutus should be found. I thank thee, Brutus,
That thou has proved Lucilius' saying true.

[3] bit

OCTAVIUS

All that served Brutus, I will entertain [4] them. 60
Fellow, wilt thou bestow thy time with me?

STRATO

Ay, if Messala will prefer [5] me to you.

OCTAVIUS

Do so, good Messala.

MESSALA

How died my master, Strato?

STRATO

I held the sword, and he did run on it.

MESSALA

Octavius, then take him to follow thee,
That did the latest service to my master.

ANTONY

This was the noblest Roman of them all.
All the conspirators save only he
Did that they did in envy of great Caesar; 70
He only, in a general honest thought
And common good to all, made one of them. [6]
His life was gentle, and the elements
So mixed in him that Nature might stand up
And say to all the world, "This was a man!"

[4] employ [5] recommend [6] *made one of them:* united
the conspirators

139

According to his virtue let us use him,
With all respect and rites of burial.
Within my tent his bones tonight shall lie,
Most like a soldier, ordered [7] honorably.
So call the field to rest, and let's away   80
To part [8] the glories of this happy day.

Exeunt omnes.

[7] treated   [8] divide